Florence Buchanan
1996

G R A P H I S   P H O T O   9 5

GRAPHIS PHOTO 95

· ·

THE INTERNATIONAL ANNUAL OF PHOTOGRAPHY

DAS INTERNATIONALE JAHRBUCH ÜBER PHOTOGRAPHIE

LE RÉPERTOIRE INTERNATIONAL DE LA PHOTOGRAPHIE

EDITED BY · HERAUSGEGEBEN VON · EDITÉ PAR:

B. MARTIN PEDERSEN

PUBLISHER AND CREATIVE DIRECTOR: B. MARTIN PEDERSEN

EDITORS: HEINKE JENSSEN, ANNETTE CRANDALL

ASSISTANT EDITOR: JÖRG REIMANN

ART DIRECTORS: B. MARTIN PEDERSEN, RANDELL PEARSON

PHOTO EDITOR: CARRE BEVILACQUA

GRAPHIS PRESS CORP. ZÜRICH (SWITZERLAND)

GRAPHIS PUBLICATIONS

GRAPHIS, THE INTERNATIONAL BI-MONTHLY JOURNAL OF VISUAL COMMUNICATION

GRAPHIS DESIGN, THE INTERNATIONAL ANNUAL OF DESIGN AND ILLUSTRATION

GRAPHIS ADVERTISING, THE INTERNATIONAL ANNUAL OF ADVERTISING

GRAPHIS BROCHURES, A COMPILATION OF BROCHURE DESIGN

GRAPHIS PHOTO, THE INTERNATIONAL ANNUAL OF PHOTOGRAPHY

GRAPHIS ALTERNATIVE PHOTOGRAPHY, THE INTERNATIONAL ANNUAL OF ALTERNATIVE PHOTOGRAPHY

GRAPHIS NUDES, A COLLECTION OF CAREFULLY SELECTED SOPHISTICATED IMAGES

GRAPHIS POSTER, THE INTERNATIONAL ANNUAL OF POSTER ART

GRAPHIS PACKAGING, AN INTERNATIONAL COMPILATION OF PACKAGING DESIGN

GRAPHIS LETTERHEAD, AN INTERNATIONAL COMPILATION OF LETTERHEAD DESIGN

GRAPHIS DIAGRAM, THE GRAPHIC VISUALIZATION OF ABSTRACT, TECHNICAL AND STATISTICAL FACTS AND FUNCTIONS

GRAPHIS LOGO, AN INTERNATIONAL COMPILATION OF LOGOS

GRAPHIS EPHEMERA, AN INTERNATIONAL COLLECTION OF PROMOTIONAL ART

GRAPHIS PUBLICATION, AN INTERNATIONAL SURVEY OF THE BEST IN MAGAZINE DESIGN

GRAPHIS ANNUAL REPORTS, AN INTERNATIONAL COMPILATION OF THE BEST DESIGNED ANNUAL REPORTS

GRAPHIS CORPORATE IDENTITY, AN INTERNATIONAL COMPILATION OF THE BEST IN CORPORATE IDENTITY DESIGN

GRAPHIS TYPOGRAPHY, AN INTERNATIONAL COMPILATION OF THE BEST IN TYPOGRAPHIC DESIGN

ART FOR SURVIVAL: THE ILLUSTRATOR AND THE ENVIRONMENT, A DOCUMENT OF ART IN THE SERVICE OF MAN.

THE GRAPHIC DESIGNER'S GREEN BOOK, ENVIRONMENTAL RESOURCES FOR THE DESIGN AND PRINT INDUSTRIES

GRAPHIS PUBLIKATIONEN

GRAPHIS, DIE INTERNATIONALE ZWEIMONATSZEITSCHRIFT DER VISUELLEN KOMMUNIKATION

GRAPHIS DESIGN, DAS INTERNATIONALE JAHRBUCH ÜBER DESIGN UND ILLUSTRATION

GRAPHIS ADVERTISING, DAS INTERNATIONALE JAHRBUCH DER WERBUNG

GRAPHIS BROCHURES, BROSCHÜRENDESIGN IM INTERNATIONAL ÜBERBLICK

GRAPHIS PHOTO, DAS INTERNATIONALE JAHRBUCH DER PHOTOGRAPHIE

GRAPHIS ALTERNATIVE PHOTOGRAPHY, DAS INTERNATIONALE JAHRBUCH ÜBER ALTERNATIVE PHOTOGRAPHIE

GRAPHIS NUDES, EINE SAMMLUNG SORGFÄLTIG AUSGEWÄHLTER AKTPHOTOGRAPHIE

GRAPHIS POSTER, DAS INTERNATIONALE JAHRBUCH DER PLAKATKUNST

GRAPHIS PACKAGING, EIN INTERNATIONALER ÜBERBLICK ÜBER DIE PACKUNGSGESTALTUNG

GRAPHIS LETTERHEAD, EIN INTERNATIONALER ÜBERBLICK ÜBER BRIEFPAPIERGESTALTUNG

GRAPHIS DIAGRAM, DIE GRAPHISCHE DARSTELLUNG ABSTRAKTER TECHNISCHER UND STATISTISCHER DATEN UND FAKTEN

GRAPHIS LOGO, EINE INTERNATIONALE AUSWAHL VON FIRMEN-LOGOS

GRAPHIS EPHEMERA, EINE INTERNATIONALE SAMMLUNG GRAPHISCHER DOKUMENTE DES TÄGLICHEN LEBENS

GRAPHIS MAGAZINDESIGN, EINE INTERNATIONALE ZUSAMMENSTELLUNG DES BESTEN ZEITSCHRIFTEN-DESIGNS

GRAPHIS ANNUAL REPORTS, EIN INTERNATIONALER ÜBERBLICK ÜBER DIE GESTALTUNG VON JAHRESBERICHTEN

GRAPHIS CORPORATE IDENTITY, EINE INTERNATIONALE AUSWAHL DES BESTEN CORPORATE IDENTITY DESIGNS

GRAPHIS TYPOGRAPHY, EINE INTERNATIONALE ZUSAMMENSTELLUNG DES BESTEN TYPOGRAPHIE DESIGN

ART FOR SURVIVAL: THE ILLUSTRATOR AND THE ENVIRONMENT, EIN DOKUMENT ÜBER DIE KUNST IM DIENSTE DES MENSCHEN

THE GRAPHIC DESIGNER'S GREEN BOOK, UMWELTKONZEPTE DER DESIGN- UND DRUCKINDUSTRIE

PUBLICATIONS GRAPHIS

GRAPHIS, LA REVUE BIMESTRIELLE INTERNATIONALE DE LA COMMUNICATION VISUELLE

GRAPHIS DESIGN, LE RÉPERTOIRE INTERNATIONAL DE LA COMMUNICATION VISUELLE

GRAPHIS ADVERTISING, LE RÉPERTOIRE INTERNATIONAL DE LA PUBLICITÉ

GRAPHIS BROCHURES, UNE COMPILATION INTERNATIONALE SUR LE DESIGN DES BROCHURES

GRAPHIS PHOTO, LE RÉPERTOIRE INTERNATIONAL DE LA PHOTOGRAPHIE

GRAPHIS ALTERNATIVE PHOTOGRAPHY, LE RÉPERTOIRE INTERNATIONAL DE LA PHOTOGRAPHIE ALTERNATIVE

GRAPHIS NUDES, UN FLORILÈGE DE LA PHOTOGRAPHIE DE NUS

GRAPHIS POSTER, LE RÉPERTOIRE INTERNATIONAL DE L'AFFICHE

GRAPHIS PACKAGING, LE RÉPERTOIRE INTERNATIONAL DE LA CRÉATION D'EMBALLAGES

GRAPHIS LETTERHEAD, LE RÉPERTOIRE INTERNATIONAL DU DESIGN DE PAPIER À LETTRES

GRAPHIS DIAGRAM, LE RÉPERTOIRE GRAPHIQUE DE FAITS ET DONNÉES ABSTRAITS, TECHNIQUES ET STATISTIQUES

GRAPHIS LOGO, LE RÉPERTOIRE INTERNATIONAL DU LOGO

GRAPHIS EPHEMERA, LE GRAPHISME – UN ÉTAT D'ESPRIT AU QUOTIDIEN

GRAPHIS PUBLICATION, LE RÉPERTOIRE INTERNATIONAL DU DESIGN DE PÉRIODIQUES

GRAPHIS ANNUAL REPORTS, PANORAMA INTERNATIONAL DU MEILLEUR DESIGN DE RAPPORTS ANNUELS D'ENTREPRISES

GRAPHIS CORPORATE IDENTITY, PANORAMA INTERNATIONAL DU MEILLEUR DESIGN D'IDENTITÉ CORPORATE

GRAPHIS TYPOGRAPHY, LE RÉPERTOIRE INTERNATIONAL DU MEILLEUR DESIGN DE TYPOGRAPHIE

ART FOR SURVIVAL: THE ILLUSTRATOR AND THE ENVIRONMENT, L'ART AU SERVICE DE LA SURVIE

THE GRAPHIC DESIGNER'S GREEN BOOK, L'ÉCOLOGIE APPLIQUÉE AU DESIGN ET À L'INDUSTRIE GRAPHIQUE

PUBLICATION NO. 244 (ISBN 3-85709-295-5)

© COPYRIGHT UNDER UNIVERSAL COPYRIGHT CONVENTION

COPYRIGHT © 1995 BY GRAPHIS PRESS CORP., DUFOURSTRASSE 107, 8008 ZURICH, SWITZERLAND

JACKET AND BOOK DESIGN COPYRIGHT © 1995 BY PEDERSEN DESIGN

141 LEXINGTON AVENUE, NEW YORK, N.Y. 10016 USA

COLOR SEPARATIONS BY DIGITAL PRE-PRESS INTERNATIONAL, SAN FRANCISCO, CA

PRINTED IN SINGAPORE BY CS GRAPHICS PTE LTD.

CONTENTS · INHALT · SOMMAIRE

REMARKS

WE EXTEND OUR HEARTFELT THANKS TO CONTRIBUTORS THROUGHOUT THE WORLD WHO HAVE MADE IT POSSIBLE TO PUBLISH A WIDE AND INTERNATIONAL SPECTRUM OF THE BEST WORK IN THIS FIELD.

ENTRY INSTRUCTIONS FOR NEXT YEAR'S ANNUAL MAY BE REQUESTED AT:
GRAPHIS PRESS
141 LEXINGTON AVENUE
NEW YORK, NY 10016-8193

ANMERKUNGEN

UNSER DANK GILT DEN EINSENDERN AUS ALLER WELT, DIE ES UNS DURCH IHRE BEI-TRÄGE ERMÖGLICHT HABEN, EIN BREITES, INTERNATIONALES SPEKTRUM DER BESTEN ARBEITEN ZU VERÖFFENTLICHEN.

TEILNAHMEBEDINGUNGEN FÜR DAS NÄCHSTE JAHRBUCH SIND ERHÄLTLICH BEIM:
GRAPHIS VERLAG AG
DUFOURSTRASSE 107
8008 ZÜRICH, SCHWEIZ

REMERCIEMENTS

NOUS REMERCIONS LES PARTICIPANTS DU MONDE ENTIER QUI ONT RENDU POSSIBLE LA PUBLICATION DE CET OUVRAGE OFFRANT UN PANORAMA COMPLET DES MEILLEURS TRA-VAUX RÉALISÉS DANS CE DOMAINE.

LES MODALITÉS D'INSCRIPTION PEUVENT ÊTRE OBTENUES AUPRÈS DE:
EDITIONS GRAPHIS
DUFOURSTRASSE 107
8008 ZÜRICH, SUISSE

(PRECEDING SPREAD) PHOTOGRAPHER: JAVIER VALLHONRAT ■ (FOLLOWING PAGE) PHOTOGRAPHER: AMY GUIP

ACKNOWLEDGEMENTS

. . . .

PRODUCTION OF THE GRAPHIS PHOTO '95 ANNUAL HAS BEEN MADE POSSIBLE BY AGFA,

A WORLDWIDE MANUFACTURER OF DIGITAL IMAGING SOLUTIONS.

AGFA ◆

FOR THE SECOND YEAR RUNNING, THIS BOOK WAS PRODUCED ENTIRELY IN A

POSTSCRIPT™ ENVIRONMENT WITH AGFA CRISTALRASTER™ TECHNOLOGY. AGFA'S IMAGESETTERS,

RIPS, FILM, CHEMISTRY, CRISTALRASTER TECHNOLOGY AND PROOFING SYSTEMS HAVE BEEN TEAMED WITH

LEADING DESKTOP PLATFORMS AND APPLICATIONS TO RAISE POSTSCRIPT COLOR

IMAGING BEYOND THAT OF TRADITIONAL PREPRESS SYSTEMS.

AS AN INDUSTRY INNOVATOR IN IMAGING TECHNOLOGY, AGFA

DRAWS ON A COMBINED EXPERIENCE IN PHOTOCHEMISTRY, ELECTRONICS AND

PRINTING TO DELIVER THE FAITHFUL REPRODUCTION OF IMAGES YOU SEE ON THESE PAGES. AGFA

CRISTALRASTER TECHNOLOGY, THE LEADING STOCHASTIC SCREENING TECHNIQUE, WAS USED

IN THE CREATION OF ALL COLOR SEPARATIONS, RESULTING IN ULTRA-FINE

RESOLUTION AND NEAR CONTINUOUS-TONE IMAGERY.

LIKE ALL PHOTOGRAPHERS, DESIGNERS, PRINTERS, AND PREPRESS PROFESSIONALS,

GRAPHIS AND AGFA CONTINUE TO SEARCH FOR THE MOST VIABLE AND REALISTIC MEANS OF REPRODUCING

ART. THIS COOPERATIVE EFFORT IS ONE MORE STEP TOWARD THAT GOAL.

SPECIAL RECOGNITION GOES TO MICHAEL PAIGE, PETER BRODERICK, AND

BRIAN ALTERIO FROM AGFA AND SANJAY SAKHUJA OF DIGITAL PRE-PRESS INTERNATIONAL

FOR THIER DEDICATION TO THE INNOVATIVE PRODUCTION OF THIS BOOK.

PRODUCTION NOTES

. . . .

SCANNER · DS 7060

INPUT RES · 300 DPI

IMAGESETTER · AVANTRA 25

RIP · AGFA STAR 800

MEDIA · AGFA ALLIANCE

CHEMISTRY · AGFA, CG50 ZEBRA

APPLICATIONS · QUARKXPRESS 3.31, PHOTOSHOPB 3.0

PLATFORM · MAC POWERPC 8100/100

PROOFING · AGFA PROOF SYSTEM 2

Press · HEIDLEBURG SPEEDMASTER 102V

INK SEQUENCE · KCMY

PAPER · 135 GRM, LEYKAM MATTE

AN INTERVIEW WITH SARAH MOON

[BY DOMINIQUE LE FUR]

Her exhibition was opening in a week and she could not grant any interviews before then. The night of the opening at the Centre National de la Photographie in Paris, Sarah Moon was constantly busy greeting all of the people who had come to congratulate her, speaking a few words with each. Models, artistic directors, photographers, and fashion magazine editors had all come to discover the exhibition and see Sarah Moon. □ Three days later, she was able to answer a few questions. On the appointed day, she was waiting for us in the privacy of her home, far from prying eyes and noisy traffic, although it is located in the center of Paris. The room was filled with flowers. A huge bouquet of white tulips occupied a place of honor on the table. As she served the first two rounds of coffee, she pointed out that she had often talked about the beginning of her career. Sarah Moon is a pseudonym, chosen when she was still a model, a time when she had already began to photograph her colleagues. "It's a shame you didn't see my video at the exhibition. In it, I explain how I began my career. Telling you about it now makes me feel like a scratched record." Her words are neither aggressive, nor weary. "At that time, taking photographs of my fellow models was a playful activity." Sarah Moon explained that she felt no bitterness about the transition from the life of a model to a different professional activity. "Sometimes, when this turning point is not negotiated well, the situation can be difficult. Life enriches you and ruins you at the same time. There is nothing you can do about it..."

DOMINIQUE LE FUR: **What does the exhibition that has just opened represent to you?**

SARAH MOON: A lot of work, 80 photographs that were presented at the last Meetings of Arles, 40 photographs of Japan, and 40 others taken since Arles. I can't really speak of it in terms of pleasure. When I look at these photographs, they remind me of the moment I took them. It is the reconstitution of both sad and happy life experiences. A part of the exhibition consists of works I realized prior to 1986, the year that Mike Yavel, my assistant and accomplice for 15 years, died.

DLF: **Could it be considered a form of recognition for your work?**

SM: Recognition comes and goes. I have a better chance of gaining recognition at my age than at the age of 20. As Jeanne Moreau said, honors come with the passing of time.

DLF: **Nevertheless, your style is remarkably constant.**

SM: I am obsessed. One doesn't change really, even if one evolves.

The themes remain, only things evolve.

DLF: **Your style is so personal, has it been copied by other photographers?**

SM: When I'm told about someone who is "copying" me, I can see the intention, but very rarely find that it resembles me. Similarly, I can recognize fake Newtons or fake Bourdins.

DLF: **Black and white is dominant in your last exhibition. Is this a deliberate choice?**

SM: Magazines demand color photographs, and fashion is done in color. However, I prefer black and white. For me, color corresponds to contract work.

DLF: **Your name is often associated with the photographs you realized for your client, Cacharel...**

I worked for the Cacharel fashion house for 20 years and 13 years for Cacharel perfumes. The contract ended two years ago. You cannot trample over your own flower bed indefinitely.

DOMINIQUE LE FUR, CHIEF EDITOR OF THE MAGAZINE *PROFESSION PHOTOGRAPHE* IN PARIS, STUDIED SOCIOLOGY BEFORE BEGINNING HIS CAREER AS A JOURNALIST FOR REGIONAL NEWSPAPERS IN BRITTANY. HE HAS BEEN A MEMBER OF SEVERAL JURIES AND PARTICIPATES IN RADIO DISCUSSIONS ON TRADITIONAL AND DIGITAL PHOTOGRAPHY.

DLF: And what if a different client in the cosmetics field offered you a contract today?

SM: It would be wonderful to start all over again with new ingredients. It would be a new adventure. However, I would also have to believe in it. In a way, I cannot do something unless I believe in it myself.

DLF: Are you interested in the new technologies such as digital photography?

SM: I have already used the Avid for commercials and discovered interesting aspects. I haven't used it for research in photography. I remain loyal to silver salts. I like these techniques, but I don't have the time to do everything. It's a bit like foreign languages: We would like to speak several, but we only speak one.

DLF: Will you be taking a few days vacation now?

SM: My vacation is my work, the pleasure and joy of taking photographs. When I am away from Paris, I take photographs. I also stroll around Paris with a camera.

DLF: What are your projects?

SM: I would like to make a movie. I made *Mississippi One* three years ago, but it wasn't a commercial success. The film interrupted my photography work, and when I came back, things had changed a little. Yes, I would like to find a story to tell that is not a story I would be able to write myself. Yes, it could be in color.

Sarah Moon was serving another round of coffee when someone rang the doorbell. Taking advantage of her absence, her cat came into the room. My long conversation with his mistress had aroused his curiosity. A minute later, Sarah Moon came back. No, our questioning had not bored her.

Another visit to her exhibition was a must. There was such a crowd on the night of the opening that we were not able to see the videos. They taught us that Sarah Moon began as a fashion and advertising photographer in 1970. Since that time she has exhibited her work regularly in Europe, Japan, and the United States. Since 1972, she has received awards for her photographs, advertising, films, and books in these same countries. A full and rich career path, traveled in simplicity. ■

Ihre Ausstellung sollte in einer Woche stattfinden, und vorher würde sie kein Interview geben können. Am Abend der Vernissage im Centre National de la Photographie in Paris scharte sich die Mode- und Photowelt um Sarah Moon, um sie zu beglückwünschen und einige Worte mit ihr zu wechseln. Mannequins, Art Direktoren, Photographen, Moderedakteurinnen waren gekommen, um die Ausstellung und Sarah Moon zu sehen.

Drei Tage später ist sie bereit zu einem Gespräch. Am vereinbarten Termin erwartet sie uns in ihrem Haus, das versteckt und abseits vom Verkehr mitten in Paris liegt. Der Salon ist voller Blumen – ein riesiger Strauss Tulpen schmückt den Tisch. Beim ersten Kaffee sagt sie, sie habe schon so oft über ihre Anfänge gesprochen. Sarah Moon ist ein Pseudonym, dass sie sich zugelegt hatte, als sie selbst noch Mannequin war und bereits anfing, ihre Kolleginnen zu photographieren. «Schade, dass Sie mein Video bei der Ausstellung nicht anschauen konnten. Ich erkläre da, wie ich begonnen habe. Wenn ich jetzt darüber spreche, komme ich mir wie eine Schallplatte mit einem Sprung vor.» In ihren Worten liegt weder Aggressivität noch Überdruss. «Damals habe ich ganz spielerisch angefangen, meine Mannequin-Kolleginnen zu photographieren.» Auf dieses Umsteigen auf eine andere Karriere angesprochen, erklärt Sarah Moon, dass sie überhaupt keine Bitterkeit empfunden habe. «Manchmal, wenn die eingeschlagene Richtung nicht gut gewählt ist, kann die Situation schwierig sein. Das Leben bereichert und zerstört den Menschen gleichzeitig, das lässt sich nicht ändern.»

DOMINIQUE LE FUR: Was bedeutet für Sie diese Ausstellung?

SARAH MOON: Viel Arbeit. 80 Photos, die bei den Rencontres d'Arles im letzten Jahr gezeigt wurden, 40 Photos aus Japan und 40 weitere, die seit Arles entstanden sind. Ich kann nicht sagen, dass es ein Vergnügen ist. Wenn ich diese Photos anschaue, erinnere ich mich an den Moment, in dem ich sie gemacht habe, an Erlebtes, das traurig und heiter zugleich war. Ein Teil der Ausstellung betrifft Aufnahmen, die vor 1986 entstanden sind, dem Jahr, in dem Mike Yavel, der 15 Jahre lang mein Assistent und Komplize war, gestorben ist.

DLF: Kann man von einer Form der Anerkennung für Ihre Arbeit sprechen?

SM: Anerkennung kommt und geht. In meinem Alter habe ich bessere Chancen, anerkannt zu werden als mit 20 Jahren. Die Ehrungen, das ist die Zeit, die vergeht, ... sagt Jeanne Moreau.

DLF: Man stellt aber eine bemerkenswerte Konstanz in Ihrer Arbeit fest.

SM: Ich bin besessen, man verändert sich nicht wirklich, auch wenn man sich entwickelt. Die Themen bleiben.

DLF: Wurde Ihr Stil von anderen Photogaphen kopiert?

SM: Wenn man mich auf jemanden hinweist, der mich «kopiert», erkenne ich zwar die Absicht, finde aber nicht, dass die Arbeit meiner ähnelt. So sehe ich auch die falschen Newtons und die Bourdins.

DLF: Schwarzweiss-Bilder dominieren in Ihrer gegenwärtigen Ausstellung. Wurde die Auswahl absichtlich so getroffen?

SM: Zeitschriften verlangen Farbe, und Mode zeigt man in Farbe, ich aber arbeite am liebsten in Schwarzweiss. Für mich bedeutet Farbe Auftragsphotographie.

DLF: Wenn man von Ihnen spricht, denkt man häufig an die Photos, die Sie für Cacharel gemacht haben.

SM: Ich habe 20 Jahre lang für Cacharel Couture gearbeitet, 13 Jahre für die Parfums. Der Vertrag ist vor zwei Jahren abgelaufen. Man kann sich nicht ständig selbst zitieren.

DLF: Und wenn eine andere Kosmetikfirma Ihnen heute eine Zusammenarbeit vorschlagen würde?

SM: Es wäre wunderbar, mit neuen Gegebenheiten neu anzufangen, ein neues Abenteuer zu beginnen. Es wäre wichtig, dass ich an die Sache glauben kann. Irgendwie kann ich nicht für etwas arbeiten, von dem ich nicht selbst überzeugt bin.

DLF: Interessieren Sie die neuen Technologien wie z.B. die digitale Photographie?

SM: Ich habe Avid schon für Werbefilme benutzt, und dabei habe ich interessante Dinge herausgefunden. Für photographische Arbeiten habe ich aber nie damit gearbeitet. Ich bleibe dem Bromsilber treu. Diese Techniken interessieren mich schon, aber ich habe nicht die Zeit, alles zu machen. Das ist wie bei den Fremdsprachen, man möchte gern mehrere sprechen, spricht aber nur eine.

DLF: Machen Sie jetzt ein paar Tage Ferien?

SM: Meine Ferien sind meine Arbeit, meine Freude am Photographieren. Wenn ich Paris verlasse, mache ich Photos.

DLF: Welche Pläne haben Sie?

SM: Ich hoffe, einen Film machen zu können. Es sind schon drei Jahre her, seit ich *Mississippi One* gemacht habe, der kein kommerzieller Erfolg geworden ist. Dieser Film hat mich von der photographischen Arbeit weggezogen, und als ich zurückkehrte, hatten sich die Dinge ein wenig verändert. Ja, ich würde gern eine Geschichte finden, die ich im Film erzählen könnte, die aber nicht meine ist.

Sarah Moon bringt noch einen Kaffee, als jemand an der Tür läutet. Diese Abwesenheit nutzt ihre Katze, um auf der Bildfläche zu erscheinen. Eine so lange Unterhaltung mit ihrer 'Herrin' hat ihre Neugier geweckt. Eine Minute später kommt Sarah Moon zurück. Nein, diese Fragen hätten sie nicht gelangweilt.

Da am Abend der Vernissage zu viele Leute da waren, besuchten wir die Ausstellung nochmal, um die Videos anzuschauen. Dabei erfuhren wir, dass Sarah Moon 1970 begonnen hat, als Mode- und Werbephotographin zu arbeiten. Seit 1970 stellt sie regelmässig in Europa, Japan und den Vereinigten Staaten aus. Seit 1972 werden ihre Photos, Arbeiten für die Werbung, Filme und Bücher in diesen Ländern mit Auszeichnungen gewürdigt. Eine Karriere voller Ereignisse und doch unkompliziert. ∎

....

DOMINIQUE LE FUR, CHEFREDAKTEUR DER ZEITSCHRIFT *PROFESSION PHOTOGRAPHE*, PARIS, BEGANN NACH EINEM SOZIOLOGIESTUDIUM ALS JOURNALIST FÜR REGIONALE TAGESZEITUNGEN IN DER BRETAGNE. ER WAR MITGLIED VERSCHIEDENER JURIES UND SPRICHT IN RADIOSENDUNGEN ÜBER DIE HERKÖMMLICHE UND DIGITALE PHOTOGRAPHIE.

Son exposition débutait dans une semaine et elle ne pouvait donner aucune interview avant cette date. Le soir du vernissage au Centre National de la Photographie à Paris, Sarah Moon n'arrêtait pas de saluer toutes les personnes qui voulaient la féliciter et lui dire quelques mots. Mannequins, directeurs artistiques, photographes, rédactrices de mode s'étaient tous donné rendez-vous pour découvrir l'exposition et voir Sarah Moon.

Trois jours plus tard, elle acceptait de répondre à quelques questions. Au jour dit, elle nous attendait dans sa maison à l'abri des regards et de la circulation bien que située en plein Paris. La salle était remplie de fleurs. Un énorme bouquet de tulipes blanches trônait sur la table. En servant les deux premiers cafés, elle fit remarquer qu'elle avait si souvent parlé de ses débuts. Sarah Moon est un pseudonyme choisi à l'époque où elle était encore mannequin et que, déjà, elle photographiait ses copines. «C'est dommage que vous n'ayez pas vu ma vidéo à l'exposition, j'y explique comment j'ai débuté. Maintenant, en en parlant, j'ai l'impression d'être un disque rayé». Aucune agressivité, aucune lassitude n'imprègnent ses porpos. «A l'époque, je photographiais de manière ludique mes collègues mannequins.» A propos de ce passage entre la vie de mannequin et une autre activité professionnelle, Sarah Moon explique qu'elle n'a ressenti aucune amertume. «Quelquefois, quand le tournant est mal pris, la situation peut être difficile. La vie vous enrichit et vous ruine en même temps, on n'y peut rien...»

DOMINIQUE LE FUR: Que représente pour vous cette exposition qui vient d'ouvrir?

SARAH MOON: Beaucoup de travail. 80 photos présentées aux dernières Rencontres d'Arles, 40 photos du Japon et 40 autres depuis Arles. Je ne peux parler d'agrément. Quand je vois ces photos, elles me rappellent le moment où je les ai prises. C'est la restitution d'un vécu triste et gai à la fois. Une partie de cette exposition est constituée de mon travail appliqué réalisé avant 1986, l'année où Mike Yavel, mon assistant et mon complice de 15 ans, est mort.

DLF: Peut-on parler d'une forme de reconnaissance pour votre travail?

SM: La reconnaissance, ça va, ça vient. A mon âge, j'ai plus de chance d'être reconnue qu'à 20 ans. Les honneurs, c'est le temps qui passe...dit Jeanne Moreau.

DLF: On note pourtant une grande constante dans votre style.

SM: Je suis obsédée, on ne change pas vraiment, même si on évolue. Les thèmes demeurent.

DLF: Votre style si personnel a-t-il été copié par d'autres photographes?

SM: Quand on me parle de quelqu'un qui me «copie», je vois l'intention mais c'est très rare que je trouve que cela me ressemble. De même, je reconnais les faux Newton ou les faux Bourdin.

DLF: Le noir et blanc domine dans votre dernière Expo, est-ce un choix délibéré?

SM: Les magazines demandent la couleur et la mode se fait en couleur mais ma préférence se porte sur le noir et blanc. La couleur correspond, pour moi, aux travaux de commande.

DLF: Votre nom est souvent associé aux photos que vous avez réalisées pour votre client Cacharel...

SM: J'ai travaillé pendant 20 ans pour Cacharel Couture, 13 ans pour les parfums. Le contrat s'est terminé il y a 2 ans. On ne peut pas piétiner ses propres plates-bandes indéfiniment.

DLF: Et si un autre client cosmétique vous proposait aujourd'hui une collaboration?

SM: Ce serait merveilleux de recommencer avec d'autres ingrédients, une nouvelle aventure. Il faudrait aussi que je puisse y croire. D'une certaine manière, je ne peux pas faire quelque chose si je n'y crois pas moi-même.

DLF: Etes-vous intéressée par les nouvelles technologies, comme la photo numérique, par exemple?

SM: J'ai déjà utilisé l'Avid pour des films publicitaires et j'y ai trouvé des choses intéressantes. Je ne m'en suis pas servi pour une recherche appliquée à la photographie. Je reste fidèle au sel d'argent. Ces techniques me plaisent mais je n'ai pas le temps de tout faire. C'est un peu comme les langues étrangères, on voudrait en parler plusieurs et on en parle une seule.

DLF: Allez-vous prendre quelques jours de vacances maintenant?

SM: Mes vacances, c'est mon travail, mon plaisir et ma joie de photographier. Quand je pars de Paris, je fais des photos. Je peux aussi me balader dans Paris avec un appareil.

DLF: Quels sont vos projets?

SM: J'espère faire un film. Cela fait maintenant trois ans que j'ai réalisé *Mississippi One* qui n'a pas été un succès commercial. Ce film a interrompu mon travail photographique et quand je suis revenue, les choses avaient un peu changé. Oui, je voudrais trouver une histoire à raconter qui ne serait pas celle que je pourrais écrire. Oui, cela pourrait être en couleur.

Sarah Moon servait un autre café quand quelqu'un sonna à la porte. Profitant de son absence, son chat arriva dans la pièce. Une si longue conversation avec sa maîtresse avait aiguisé sa curiosité. Une minute plus tard, Sarah Moon revint. Non, ces questions ne l'avaient pas ennuyée.

Une autre visite à son exposition s'imposait car la foule, le soir du vernissage, ne nous avait pas permis de regarder les vidéos. Elles nous apprirent que Sarah Moon a débuté comme photographe de mode et de publicité en 1970. Elle expose régulièrement en Europe, au Japon et aux Etats-Unis. Depuis 1972, elle est récompensée pour ses photos, ses publicités, ses films et ses livres dans ces mêmes pays. Un itinéraire plutôt chargé, mais en toute simplicité. ∎

DOMINIQUE LE FUR, RÉDACTEUR EN CHEF DU MAGAZINE *PROFESSION PHOTOGRAPHE* PARIS, A DÉBUTÉ DANS LA PRESSE QUOTIDIENNE RÉGIONALE EN BRETAGNE APRÈS DES ÉTUDES DE SOCIOLOGIE. MEMBRE DE DIFFÉRENTS JURY, IL PARTICIPE À DES ÉMISSIONS DE RADIO SUR LA PHOTO ARGENTIQUE ET NUMÉRIQUE.

Preceding Spread: Kenji Toma | Above: Enrique Badulescu | Opposite: Michael Zeppetello

Enrique Badulescu

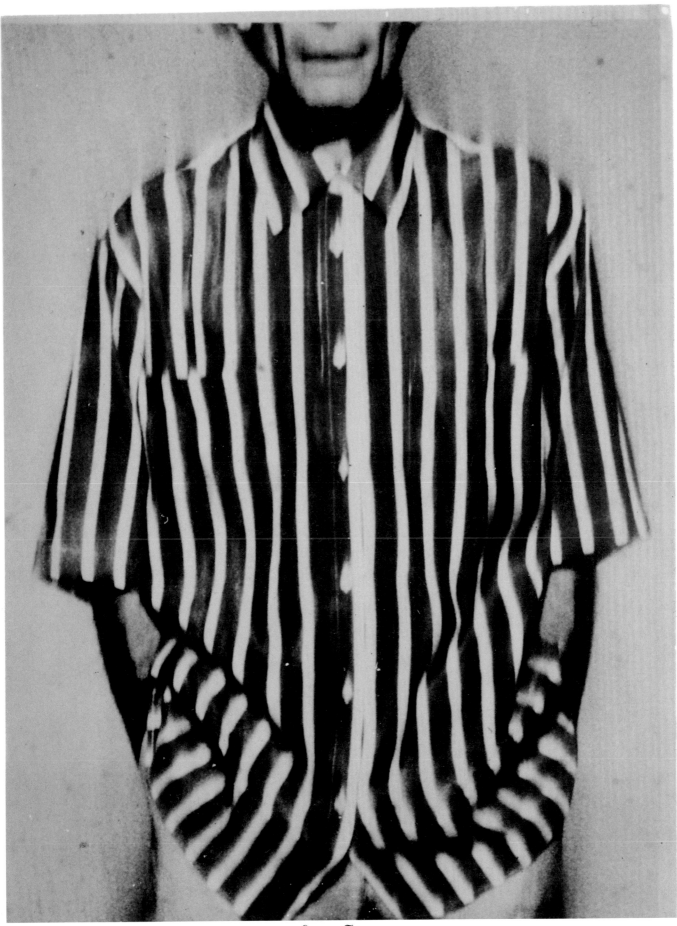

ENRIQUE BADULESCU

Enrique Badulescu

Thomas Schenk

Above: Enrique Badulescu | Opposite: Satoshi Saikusa

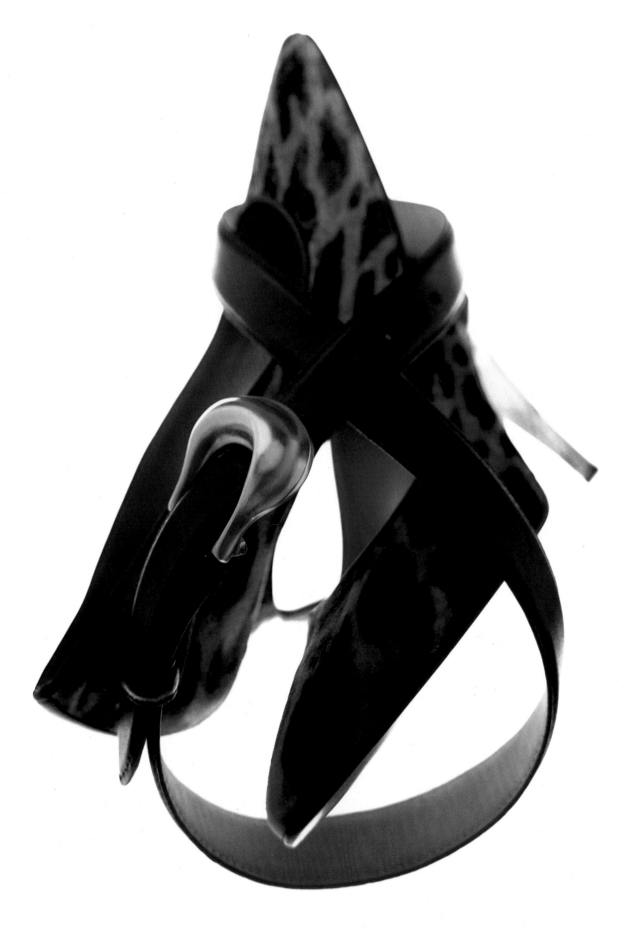

Kenji Toma

Kenji Toma

Kenji Toma

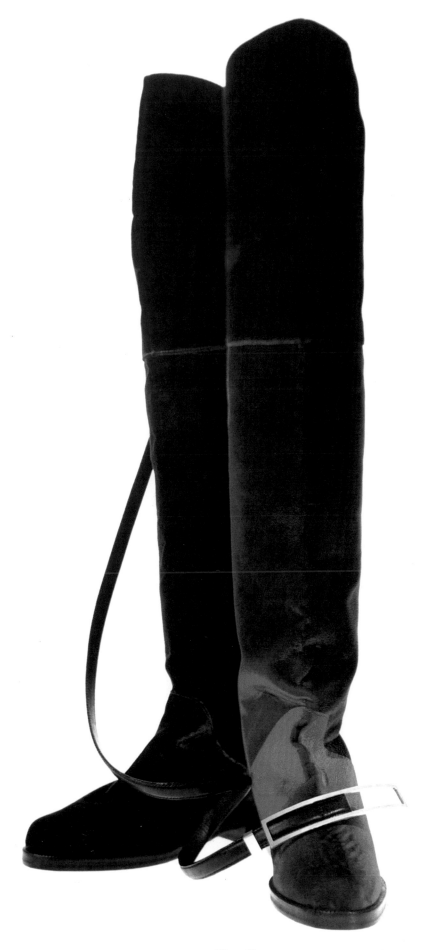

Kenji Toma

Rodney Smith

Steven Meisel

Opposite: Nick Knight | Above: Gilles Hancock

ELLEN VON UNWERTH

Peter Lindbergh

This Spread: Sarah Moon

Rineke Dijkstra

Michel Comte

Juergen Teller

Fridhelm Volk

Above: Rachel Jerome | Opposite: Klaus Mitteldorf

Aldo Fallai

Arthur Elgort

Rodney Smith

ELLEN VON UNWERTH

Above: Dominique Ddieulot | Opposite: Nadav Kander

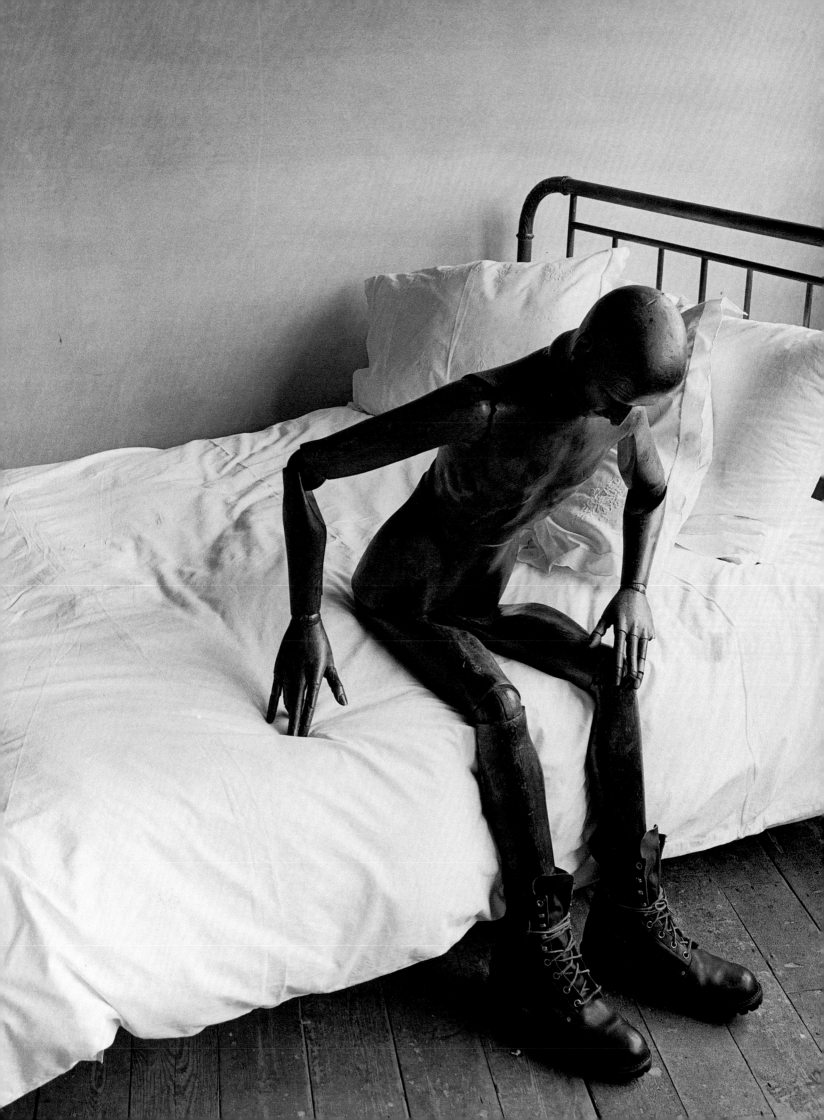

Mario Testino

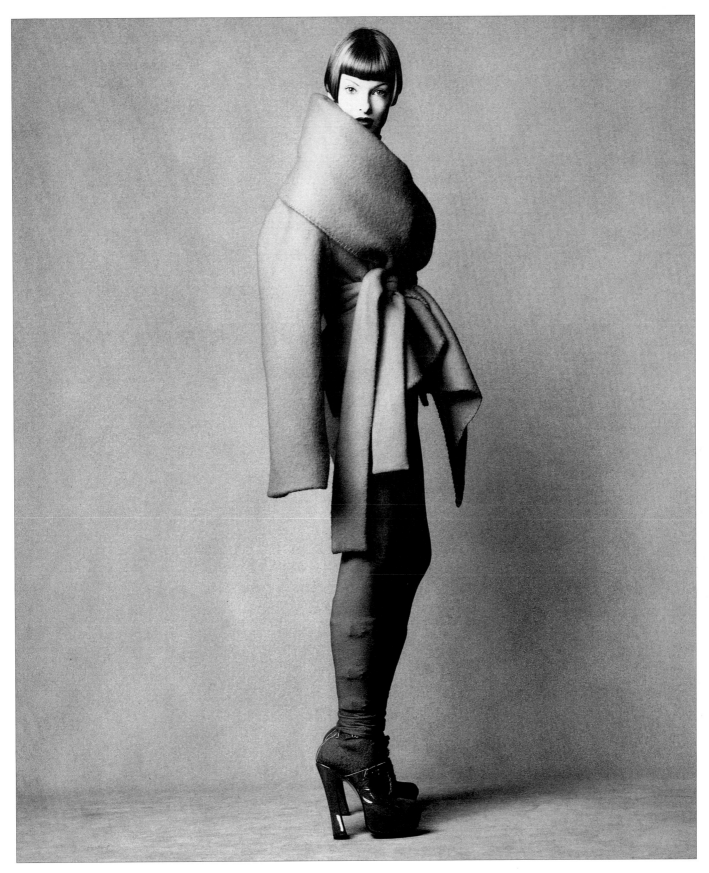

Steven Meisel

HERB RITTS

Herb Ritts

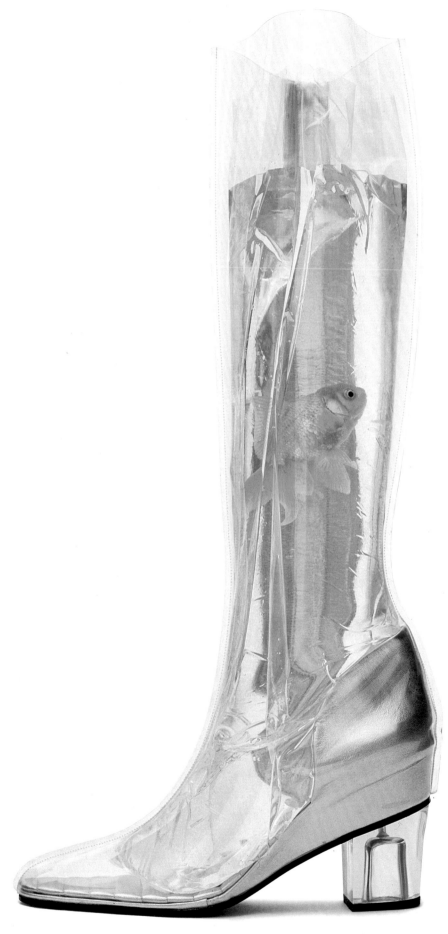

Thomas Schenk

Javier Vallhonrat

Above: Mario Testino / Opposite: Bob Frame

This Spread: Nadav Kander

JOURNALISM

JOURNALISMUS

JOURNALISME

(PAGE 60 AND THIS SPREAD) PHOTOGRAPHER: LOIS LAMMERHUBER REPRESENTATIVE: PHOTOARCHIVE LAMMERHUBER PUBLISHER/CLIENT: *GEO*/GRUNER + JAHR CAMERA: NIKON F4 FILM: KODAK EKTACHROME 100 EPN ART DIRECTOR: ERWIN EHRET PICTURE EDITOR: NELE BRAAS COUNTRY: GERMANY ■ JERUSALEM, 4000 YEARS OLD, IS HOLY FOR CHRISTIANS, JEWS, AND MUSLIMS; JEWS AND PALESTINIANS CONSIDER IT THEIR CAPITAL. INDEED, JERUSALEM IS THE MOST CRITICAL PLACE FOR THE WHOLE PEACE PROCESS. ❑ (PAGE 60) CHILDREN IN AN ARAB SUBURB USE A DESTROYED CAR AS A PLAYGROUND. ❑ (OPPOSITE PAGE FROM TOP TO BOTTOM AND FROM LEFT TO RIGHT) ISRAELI GUARD STATION AT THE TOP OF THE WESTERN WALL; FIRST PAGE OF THE KORAN IN AN ARAB SCHOOL DISTRICT; JEWS CELEBRATING THE FESTIVAL OF THORA (THE PLASTIC PROTECTS THE READER AGAINST THE RAIN); OLD CITY BILLIARD CAFÉ; DEMONSTRATION FOR PALESTINIAN PRISONERS; OLD CITY SOUK CAFÉ. ❑ (THIS PAGE) A CHRISTIAN WOMAN FROM ETHIOPIA IN THE CRYPT OF JESUS CHRIST BENDING ON A STONE PLATE WHERE JESUS IS SAID TO HAVE BEEN ANOINTED BEFORE HIS BURIAL. ● JERUSALEM, 4000 JAHRE ALT, HEILIG FÜR CHRISTEN, JUDEN UND MOSLEMS UND VON JUDEN UND PALÄSTI-NENSERN ALS HAUPTSTADT BEANSPRUCHT. HIER WIRD SICH DIE ENTWICKLUNG DES FRIEDENSPROZESSES ENTSCHEIDEN. ❑ (SEITE 60) KINDER IN EINER ARABISCHEN VORSTADT TURNEN AUF EINEM WÄHREND DER INTIFADA ZERSTÖRTEN AUTO. ❑ (GEGENÜBER VON

OBEN LINKS NACH UNTEN RECHTS) ISRAELISCHE WACHSTATION OBEN AUF DER WESTLICHEN MAUER; DIE ERSTE SEITE DES KORANS, IN EINEM ARABISCHEN SCHULDISTRIKT; JUDEN FEIERN DAS THORA-FEST (DIE PLASTIKPLANE SCHÜTZT DEN VORLESENDEN VOR DEM REGEN; BILLARD-CAFÉ IN DER ALTSTADT; DEMONSTRATION FÜR PALÄSTINENSISCHE GEFANGENE; SOUK-CAFÉ IN DER ALTSTADT. ❑ (DIESE SEITE) EINE ÄTHIOPISCHE CHRISTIN SCHMIEGT IHRE WANGE AN DIE STEINPLATTE IN DER GRABESKIRCHE CHRISTI, AUF DER DER GEKREUZIGTE VOR SEINER BESTATTUNG GESALBT WORDEN SEIN SOLL. ▲ VIEILLE DE 4000 ANS, LA VILLE DE JÉRUSALEM, LIEU SAINT POUR LES CHRÉTIENS, LES JUIFS ET LES MUSULMANS, EST AU CŒUR DES DISSENSIONS QUI OPPOSENT JUIFS ET PALESTINIENS DANS LE DÉLICAT PROCESSUS DE PAIX. ❑ (PAGE 60) UNE CARCASSE DE VOITURE SERT DE «TERRAIN DE JEU» AUX ENFANTS D'UNE BANLIEUE ARABE. ❑ (PAGE CI-CONTRE DE HAUT EN BAS ET DE GAUCHE À DROITE) UN POSTE DE GARDE ISRAÉLIEN SITUÉ SUR LE MUR OUEST; LA PREMIÈRE PAGE DU CORAN DANS UNE ÉCOLE DU QUARTIER ARABE; JUIFS EN TRAIN DE FÊTER LA THORA (DES BÂCHES DE PLASTIQUE PROTÈGENT L'ORATEUR DE LA PLUIE); CAFÉ AVEC BILLARD DANS LE VIEUX JÉRUSALEM; MA-NIFESTATION POUR DES PRISONNIERS PALESTINIENS; CAFÉ DU SOUK DANS LA VIEILLE VILLE. ❑ (CI-DESSUS) UNE CHRÉTIENNE ORIGINAIRE D'ÉTHIOPIE SE RECUEILLE SUR LA DALLE DE LA CRYPTE OÙ LE CHRIST AURAIT ÉTÉ OINT AVANT D'ÊTRE INHUMÉ.

PHOTOGRAPHER: TOM STODDART PUBLISHER/CLIENT: VOGUE/CONDÉ NAST PUBLICATION INC. COUNTRY: USA ■ SCENES FROM SARAJEVO: (THIS SPREAD LEFT) FATIMA KAFEDZIC, A MUSLIM MOTHER AND CHARITY WORKER, DRIES OFF ONE OF HER TEN CHILDREN; (THIS SPREAD RIGHT) GORDANA KNEZEVIC, DEPUTY EDITOR OF SARAJEVO'S NEWSPAPER OSLOBODENJE, AMID THE NEW GRAVES AT LION CEMETERY. THE PHOTOS BELONG TO AN ARTICLE ENTITLED "WOMEN UNDER FIRE" IN AMERICAN VOGUE. ● SZENEN AUS SARAJEWO: (DIESE DOPPELSEITE LINKS) FATIMA KAFEDZIC, EINE MUSLEMIN, MUTTER UND SOZIALARBEITERIN, BEIM ABTROCKNEN EINES IHRER ZEHN KINDER; (DIESE DOPPELSEITE RECHTS) GORDONA KNEZEVIC, STELLVERTRETENDE

CHEFREDAKTEURIN DER ZEITUNG OSLOBODENJE IN SARAJEWO, INMITTEN VON FRISCHEN GRÄBERN DER KRIEGSOPFER IN SARAJEWO. DIE BILDER GEHÖREN ZU EINEM BEITRAG UNTER DEM TITEL «FRAUEN UNTER BESCHUSS» IN DER AMERIKANISCHEN VOGUE. ▲ SCÈNES DE SARAJEVO: À GAUCHE, FATIMA KAFEDZIC, UNE MUSULMANE, MÈRE DE FAMILLE ET ASSISTANTE SOCIALE, EN TRAIN DE SÉCHER L'UN DE SES DIX ENFANTS; À DROITE, GORDONA KNEZEVIC, RÉDACTRICE EN CHEF ADJOINTE DU JOURNAL OSLOBODENJE À SARAJEVO, AU MILIEU DES TOMBES FRAÎCHEMENT CREUSÉES DES VICTIMES DE LA GUERRE. CES IMAGES ILLUS- TRAIENT UN ARTICLE PUBLIÉ DANS L'ÉDITION AMÉRICAINE DE VOGUE ET INTITULÉ «FEMMES SOUS LES TIRS D'OBUS».

(THIS PAGE) PHOTOGRAPHER: ARTHUR THILL REPRESENTATIVE: A.T.P. COUNTRY: GERMANY ■ THE BENETTON BOX AT HOCKENHEIM BURNING. THIS PHOTO WON THE BEST PRESS SPORTS PHOTO AWARD OF THE SSF WORLD PHOTO CONTEST 95 (JAPAN AS WELL AS THE THIRD PRIZE IN THE CATEGORY SPORT/STORIES OF THE 38TH WORLD PRESS PHOTO CONTEST. ● (DIESE SEITE) DER BENETTON-BOXENBRAND IN HOCKENHEIM. DIE AUFNAHME WURDE BEIM SSF WORLD SPORTS PHOTO CONTEST 95 IN JAPAN ALS BESTES SPORTPRESSEPHOTO AUSGEZEICHNET. AUSSERDEM ERHIELT ES DEN DRITTEN PREIS BEIM 38. WORLD PRESS PHOTO CONTEST IN DER KATEGORIE SPORT/STORIES. ▲ (CI-DESSOUS) LE STAND DE L'ÉCURIE BENETTON EN FLAMMES SUR LE CIRCUIT D'HOCKENHEIM. LORS DU SSF WORLD SPORTS PHOTO CONTEST 95, CETTE PHOTO REÇUT LE PRIX DE LA MEILLEURE PHOTOGRAPHIE DE PRESSE DANS LA CATÉGORIE «SPORTS». EN OUTRE, ELLE A DÉCROCHÉ LE TROISIÈME PRIX LORS DU 38.

WORLD PRESS PHOTO CONTEST DANS LA CATÉGORIE «SPORT/STORIES». ■ (OPPOSITE PAGE) PHOTOGRAPHER: PAUL LOWE REPRESENTATIVE: NETWORK PHOTOGRAPHERS LTD. PUBLISHER/CLIENT: AVENUE/DE GEILLUSTREERDE PERS BV ART DIRECTOR: HANS VAN BLOMMESTEIN COUNTRY: NETHERLANDS ■ (OPPOSITE) SOMALIA, 1992. THE CHILDREN HERE WERE NOT WAITING FOR FOOD DISTRIBUTION; THEY WERE FENCED IN. THEIR LOOKS HAUNTED THE PHOTOGRAPHER, WHO HAD TO ASK HIMSELF IF, AS A PHOTOGRAPHER, HE IS JUST A VOYEUR—ALWAYS CLOSE TO THE ACTION BUT NEVER REALLY TAKING ACTION HIMSELF. ● (GEGENÜBER) SOMALIA, 1992. DIE KINDER WARTETEN NICHT AUF DIE VERTEILUNG VON NAHRUNGSMITTELN, SIE WAREN IM WAHRSTEN SINNE AUSGESCHLOSSEN. IHR BLICK VERFOLGTE DEN PHOTOGRAPHEN: «SIND WIR NICHT NUR VOYEURE, IMMER NAH AM ORT DER HANDLUNG, OHNE SELBST EINZUGREIFEN?» ▲ (CI-CONTRE) SOMALIE, 1992. CES ENFANTS N'ATTENDAIENT

PAS UNE DISTRIBUTION DE VIVRES, MAIS ÉTAIENT TOUT BONNEMENT EXCLUS. LEUR REGARD HANTA LONGTEMPS LE PHO-
TOGRAPHE QUI SE DEMANDA S'IL N'ÉTAIT PAS QU'UN VOYEUR TOUJOURS PROCHE, MAIS JAMAIS AU CŒUR DE L'ACTION. ■
(PAGE 68) PHOTOGRAPHER: BORIS MIKHAILOV REPRESENTATIVE: ALEXANDER SHOUMOV GALLERY: XL GALLERY COUNTRY: RUSSIA ■ (PAGE
68) A SERIES OF PHOTOGRAPHS SHOWING EVERYDAY LIFE IN SMALL TOWNS IN DIFFERENT PARTS OF THE FORMER SOVIET UNION,
A TALK ON LIFE IN GENERAL. HE TOOK HIS IMAGES AT CHILD'S EYE LEVEL. ● (SEITE 68) EINE REIHE VON BILDERN DES
TÄGLICHEN LEBENS AN VERSCHIEDENEN ORTEN DER EHEMALIGEN SOWJETUNION. DER PHOTOGRAPH BORIS MIKHAILOV NENNT ES
EINE REPORTAGE MIT ASSOZIATIVEM CHARAKTER, EIN GESPRÄCH ÜBER DAS LEBEN IM ALLGEMEINEN. ER MACHTE SEINE
AUFNAHMEN AUS DER PERSPEKTIVE EINES KINDES. ▲ (PAGE 68) SÉRIE D'IMAGES ILLUSTRANT LA VIE QUOTIDIENNE DANS DIVERS

ENDROITS DE L'ANCIENNE UNION SOVIÉTIQUE. POUR LE PHOTOGRAPHE BORIS MIKHAILOV, C'EST UN REPORTAGE À CARACTÉRE
ASSOCIATIF, UN DISCOURS SUR LA VIE EN GÉNÉRAL. IL A PRIS SES PHOTOS DE LA «PERSPECTIVE D'UN ENFANT». ■ (PAGE 69)
PHOTOGRAPHER: JONATHAN DiPIPPO CAMERA: HASSELBLAD 6X6 FILM: T-MAX 400 COUNTRY: USA ■ (PAGE 69, TOP LEFT) A 50-POUND
KING SALMON TAKEN FROM THE YUKON RIVER, JUNE 1994. THE MAN IS AN ATHABASCAN INDIAN FROM THE ALASKAN VILLAGE OF
GRAYLING. THE PHOTOGRAPHER WAS STRUCK BY THE POWER OF THE FISH AND THE WAY THE MAN'S BODY ACTED AS A PEDESTAL
ON WHICH TO DISPLAY IT. (TOP RIGHT AND BOTTOM LEFT) SISTERS IN CHITINA ALASKA, MAY 1994. THE PHOTOGRAPHER WAS
WALKING THROUGH THE TINY TOWN AND CAME ACROSS THESE GIRLS PLAYING IN THEIR FRONT YARD. HE THOUGHT THEY SEEMED
TO BE ACTING OUT SOME STRANGE RITUAL OR BIZARRE PERFORMANCE WHEN ACTUALLY THEY WERE JUST PLAYING IN THE YARD.

(BOTTOM RIGHT) THE DAY AFTER A FIGHT WITH A DRUNK DRIVER, TALKEETNA, ALASKA, JUNE 1994. THIS MAN TRIED TO STOP A DRUNK MAN FROM DRIVING HOME, WHICH RESULTED IN A FIGHT. ● (OBEN LINKS) EIN CA. 45 PFUND SCHWERER KÖNIGSLACHS AUS DEM YUKON-FLUSS. DER MANN IST EIN ATHAPASKA-INDIANER AUS EINEM DORF IN ALASKA. DER MÄCHTIGE FISCH, DARGEBOTEN AUF DEM KÖRPER DES INDIANERS, FASZINIERTE DEN PHOTOGRAPHEN. (OBEN RECHTS UND UNTEN LINKS) SCHWESTERN IN CHITINA, ALASKA, MAI 1994. WAS AUF DEN PHOTOGRAPHEN WIE EIN SELTSAMES RITUAL WIRKTE, WAR EIN EINFACHES SPIEL. (UNTEN RECHTS) DER VERSUCH, EINEN BETRUNKENEN VOM AUTOFAHREN ABZUHALTEN, ENDETE IN EINER PRÜGELEI. DAS OPFER

AM TAG DANACH. TALKEETNA, ALASKA, JUNI 1994. ▲ (EN HAUT À GAUCHE) UN SAUMON ROYAL D'ENV. 25 KILOS PÊCHÉ DANS LE FLEUVE YUKON, JUIN 1994. L'HOMME EST UN INDIEN ATHABASCA D'UN VILLAGE DE L'ALASKA. LE PHOTOGRAPHE FUT FASCINÉ PAR LA PUISSANCE DU POISSON ET LA MANIÈRE DE LE PRÉSENTER, LE CORPS DE L'HOMME FAISANT OFFICE DE PIÉDESTAL. (EN HAUT À DROITE ET EN-BAS À GAUCHE) SŒURS PHOTOGRAPHIÉES À CHITINA, ALASKA, MAI 1994. CE QUE LE PHOTOGRAPHE PRIT POUR UN ÉTRANGE RITUEL S'AVÉRA ÊTRE EN FAIT UN SIMPLE JEU D'ENFANTS. (EN-BAS À DROITE) LA TENTATIVE D'EMPÊCHER UN HOMME IVRE DE PRENDRE LE VOLANT SE TERMINA EN BAGARRE. LA VICTIME, LE LENDEMAIN, TALKEETNA, ALASKA, JUIN 1994.

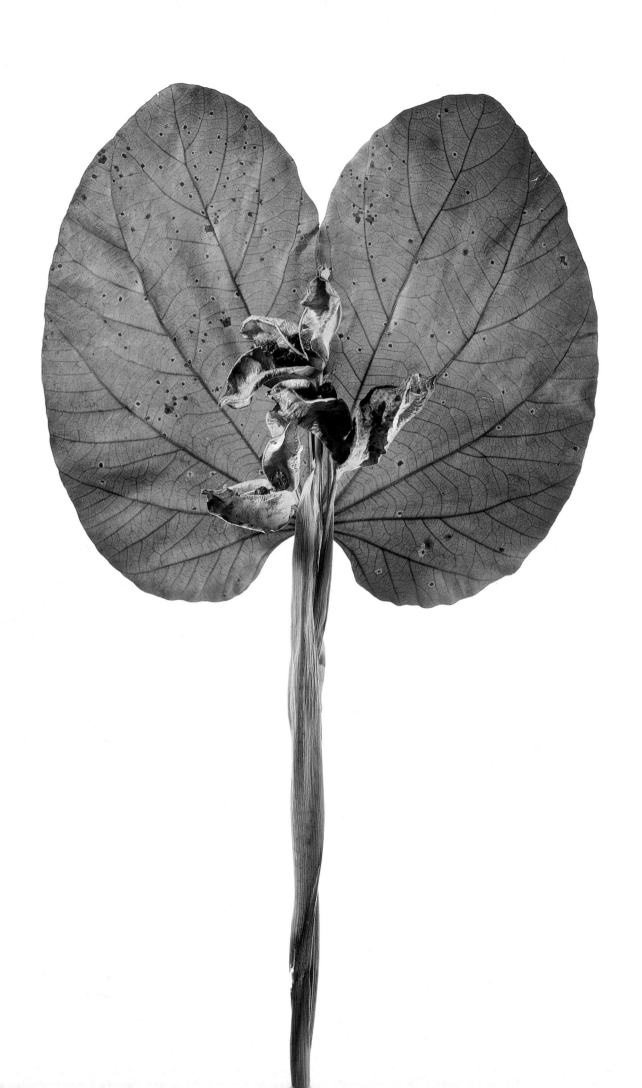

STILL LIFE

STILLEBEN

NATURE MORTE

Preceding Spread and Opposite: Gerd Aumeier / Above: Andrea Gentl, Marty Hyers

LISA SPINDLER

Mark Laita

Above: Imre Gabor Eck | Opposite: André Baranowski | Following Spread: Sigurd Kranendonk

Ricardo de Vicq de Cumptich

CRAIG CUTLER

Above: Craig Cutler | Opposite: Kathryn Kleinman

Walter Colley

Robert Tardio

Jenny Lynn

Jennifer Baumann

FOOD

LEBENSMITTEL

CUISINE

Preceding Spread: Lizzie Himmel | Above: Sigurd Kranendonk

Top: Joyce Oudkerk Pool / Bottom: Deborah Jones

Rosanne Olson

Above: Sigurd Kranendonk | Following Spread: Johan De Boer

Rosanne Olson

Jörn Zolondek

Christian von Alvensleben

Thomas Schüpping

PORTRAITS

MENSCHEN

PERSONNES

Preceding Spread: Ludovic Moulin | Above: Michele Clement

Michele Clement

Barbara Bordnick

Ron Bambridge

Ron Bambridge

Howard Schatz

Manolo Garcia

Peggy Sirota © British Vogue, The Conde Nast Publications Ltd.

Aernout Overbeeke

Aernout Overbeeke

David Powers

Steve Marsel

José Picayo

Kent Barker

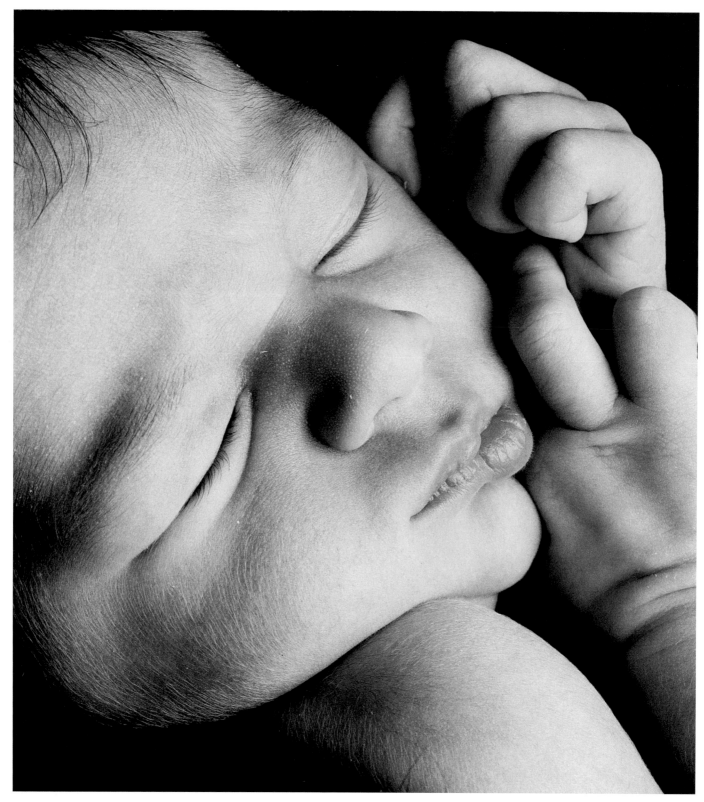

Marc Norberg

Lisa Spindler

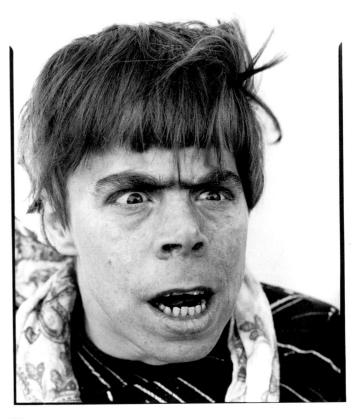

Abhijit Varde

Harry De Zitter

Herb Ritts

Herb Ritts

Marc Norberg

Ron Baxter Smith

Rosanne Olson

Mark Hanauer

Terry Husebye

BOB FRAME

Stephanie Pfriender

Dennis Manarchy

Achim Deterding

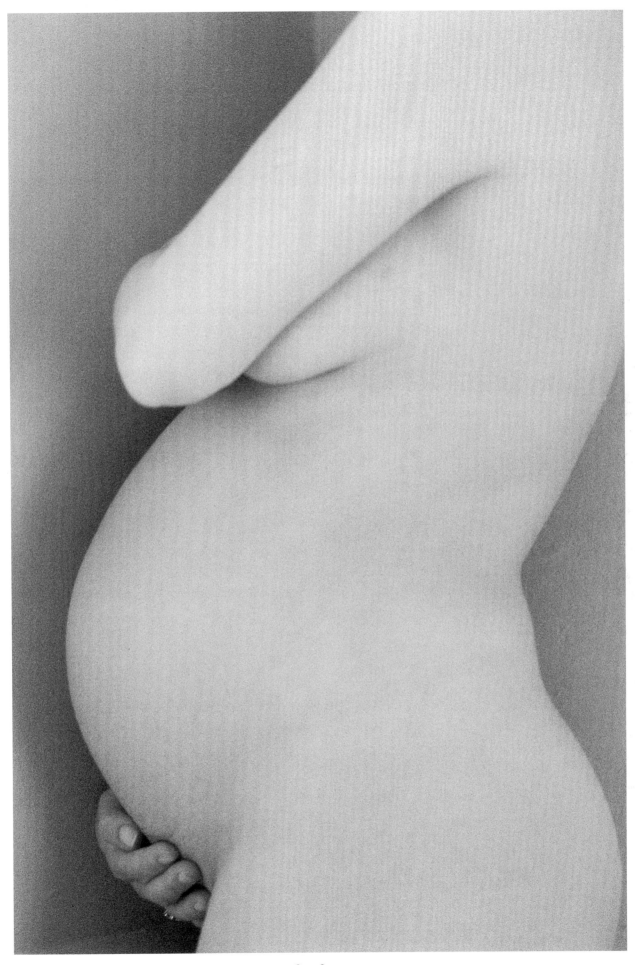

Lisa Spindler

Dieter Blum

Peter Kelih

Mark Seliger

MARK SELIGER

Above: Howard Schatz | Opposite: Kenji Toma

Neil Beckerman

Dan Borris

Above: Enrique Badulescu / Opposite: Fabrizio Ferri

RJ Muna

Lisa Spindler

Above: George Petrakes | Opposite: Mark Seliger

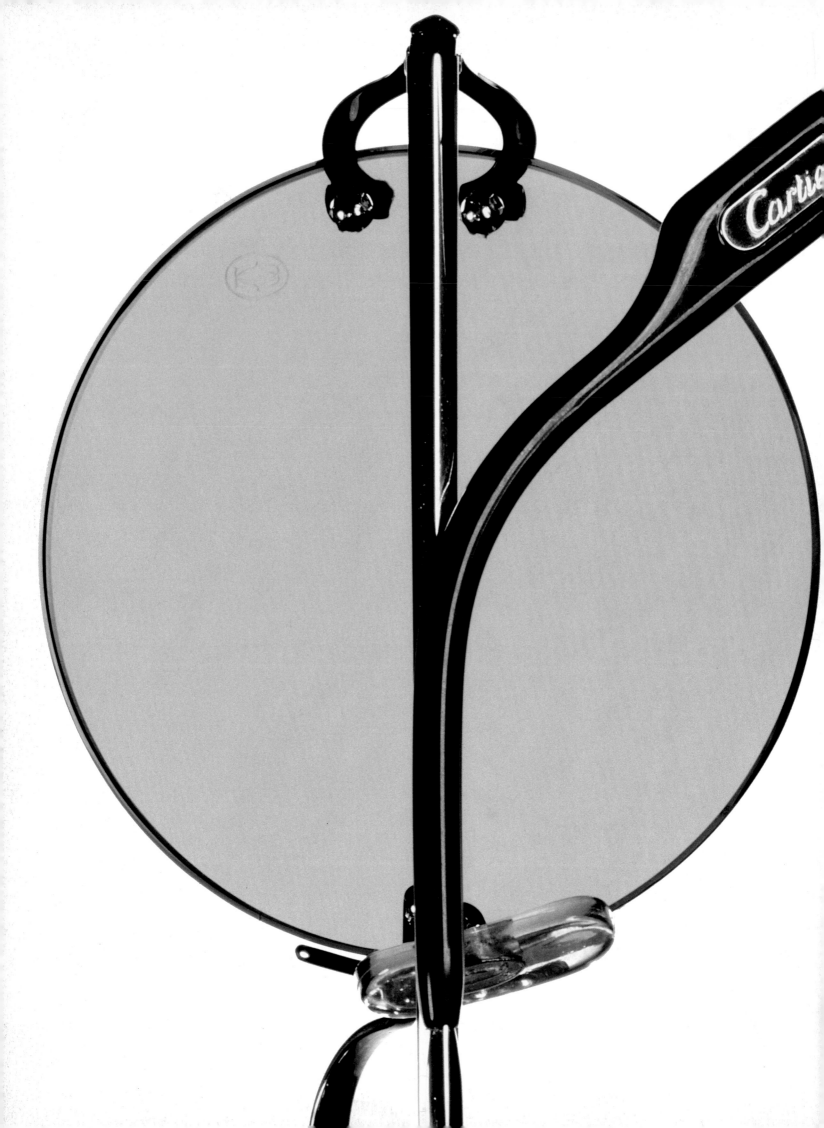

PRODUCTS

SACHAUFNAHMEN

PRODUITS

Preceding Spread: Richard J. Burbridge / Above: Conny J. Winter

Conny J. Winter

Natalie Boehm

Ron Fehling

Rian Horn

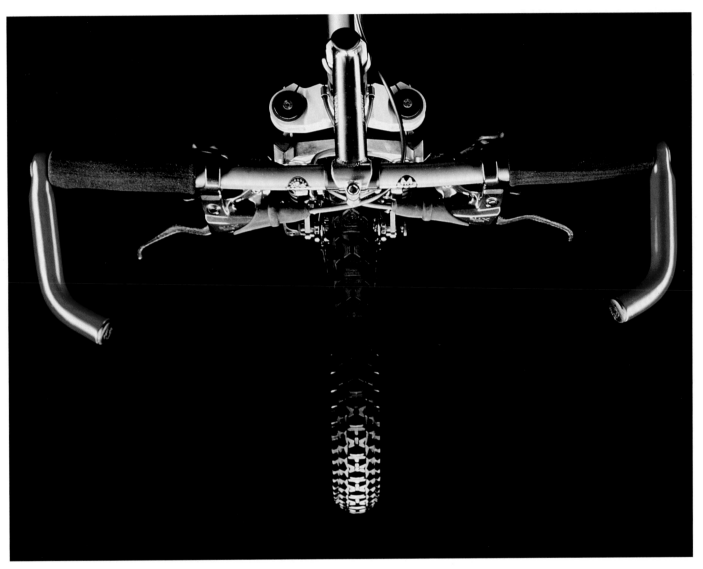

Dörfel & Kuhn Fotodesign

LANDSCAPES

LANDSCHAFTEN

PAYSAGES

Preceding Spread: Harry De Zitter | Above: Intae Kim

Intae Kim

PETER ECKERT

Mike Salisbury

Kent Barker

Fabrizio Ferri

Aernout Overbeeke

Christopher Thomas

Sally Gall

Kent Barker

Opposite: Steve Richardson | Above: Les Szurkowski

Klaus D. Francke

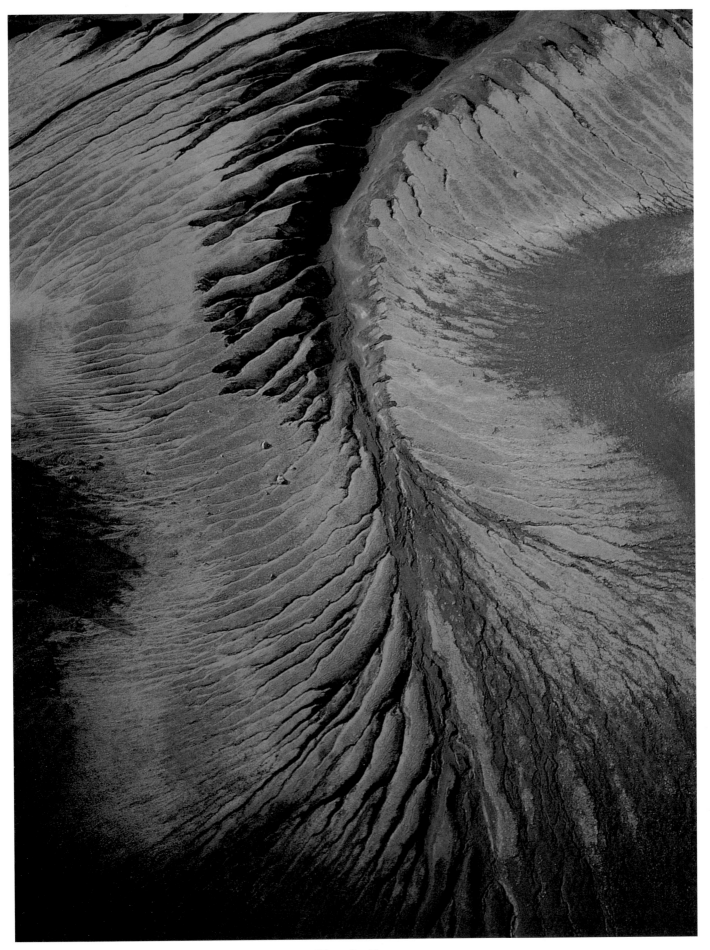

Klaus D. Francke

This Spread: Klaus D. Francke

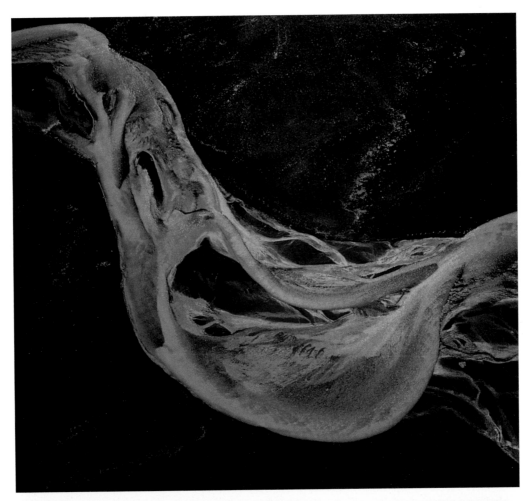

STEPHEN WILKES

Nadav Kander

ARCHITECTURE

ARCHITEKTUR

ARCHITECTURE

Preceding Spread: Armin Buhl / Above: Michael Melford

Michael Melford

Aernout Overbeeke

Aernout Overbeeke

Aernout Overbeeke

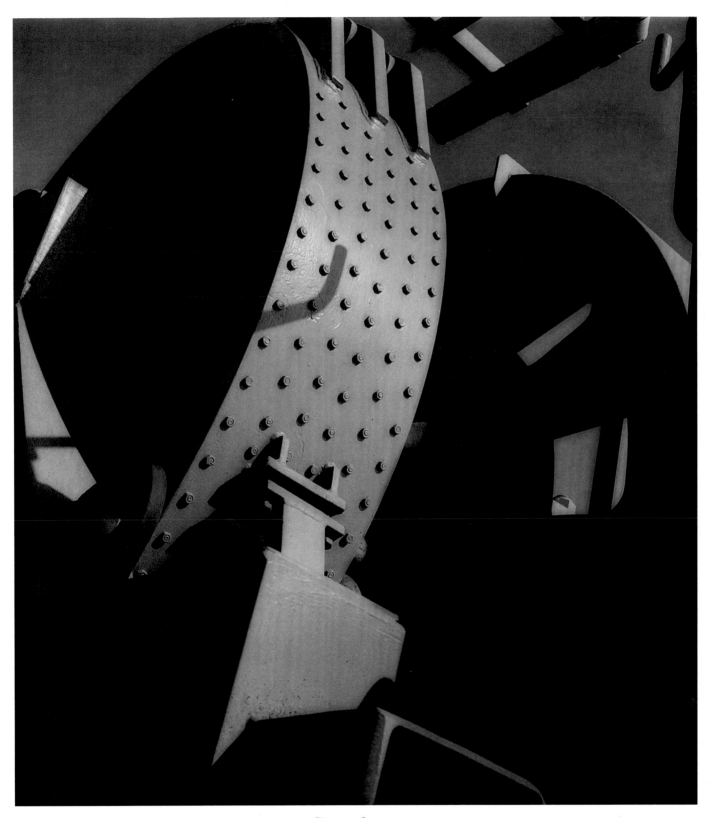

Aernout Overbeeke

Virgile Bertrand

Virgile Bertrand

Virgile Bertrand

Frances Mocnik

Frances Mocnik

This Spread: François Halard

Joanne Dugan

Peter Eckert

WILDLIFE

TIERE

ANIMAUX

Preceding Spread: Martyn Colbeck / Above: Oliver Meckes

Oliver Meckes

Bruce Weber

James Schnepf

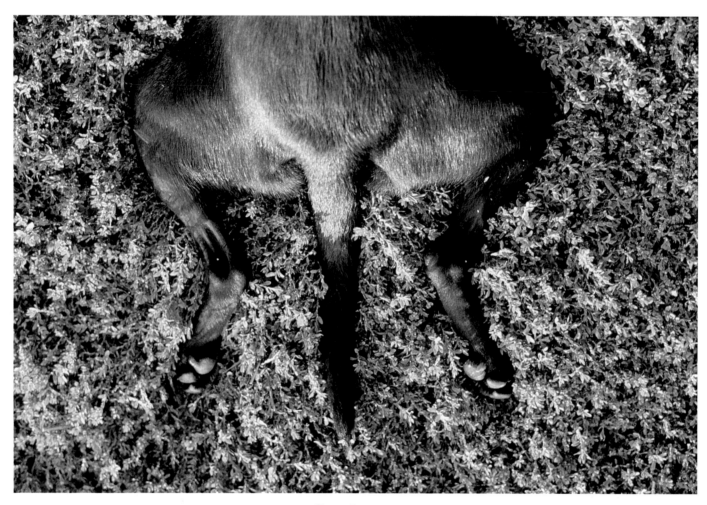

Philip Derendorf

Dirk Fischer

SPORTS

SPORT

SPORT

Preceding Spread: Johnathon Abrielle | Above: The Douglas Brothers

John Huet

COVER (Front and back) Photographer: SARAH MOON Representative: BARBARA VON SCHREIBER Publisher: *New York Times Magazine* Camera: POLAROID Film: POLAROID Art Director: JANET FROELICH Designer: CATHY GILMORE-BARNES Stylist: FRANS ANKONE Country: USA

PAGE 2 Photographer: JAVIER VALLHONRAT Representative: MICHELE FILOMENO Client: Jhon Galiano SPAIN Country: SPAIN

PAGE 4 Photographer: AMY GUIP Country: USA

PAGE 16 Photographer: KENJI TOMA Representative: MICHAEL ASH Client: CHIC SIMPLE Camera: MAMIYA 6x7 Film: KODAK VPS Art Director: ROBERT VALENTINE Producers: JEFF STONE, KIM JOHNSON Country: USA ■ Photograph from the book *Chic Simple: Body*. The focus of this shot is the lipstick smudged on the teeth. ● Aufnahme aus *Chic Simple: Body*, ein Schönheitsbuch. Hier geht es um den Lippenstift. ▲ Photo extraite de *Chic Simple: Body*, un livre sur la beauté. Ici, le rouge à lèvres tient la vedette.

PAGE 18 Photographer: ENRIQUE BADULESCU Representatives: GIOVANNI TESTINO USA, MICHELE FILOMENO, EUROPE Publisher/Client: *HARPER'S BAZAAR*/THE HEARST CORPORATION Camera: PENTAX 6x7 Film: FUJI Art Director: FABIEN BARON Stylist: SCIASCIA GAMBACCINI Country: USA ■ Swimwear presented in *Harper's Bazaar*. ● Bademode, für *Harper's Bazaar* photographiert. ▲ Maillots de bain présentés dans *Harper's Bazaar*.

PAGE 19 Photographer: MICHAEL ZEPPETELLO Representative: STOCKLAND MARTEL Publisher/Client: *ANNA* MAGAZINE/RIZZOLI Art Director/Editor: MARINA MALAVASI Country: USA ■ Photograph entitled "Scrunch face," published in *Anna* magazine. ● «Scrunch Face» (Grimasse) – Aufnahme für die Zeitschrift *Anna*. ▲ «Scrunch Face» – Cette «grimace» fut publiée dans le magazine *Anna*.

PAGE 20 Photographer: ENRIQUE BADULESCU Representatives: GIOVANNI TESTINO Publisher/Client: *VOGUE PARIS*/CONDÉ NAST Camera: PENTAX BACK Film: FUJI FP Art Director: DONALD SCHNEIDER Stylist: DELPHIN TREANTON Country: USA ■ Fashion photograph taken for *Vogue Paris*. ● Modeaufnahme für *Vogue Paris*. ▲ Photo de mode publiée dans *Vogue Paris*.

PAGE 21 Photographer: ENRIQUE BADULESCU Representative: CAMILLA LOWTHER Client: CHARLIE WATTS/THE ROLLING STONES Camera: LEICA Art Director: JOHN WARWICKER Designer: PAUL SMITH Country: USA ■ Photo used on a record cover for the Rolling Stones. ● Diese Aufnahme wurde für eine Platte der Rolling Stones verwendet. ▲ Cette photo illustre le boîtier d'un CD des Rolling Stones.

PAGE 22 Photographer: THOMAS SCHENK Publisher/Client: *AVENUE*/DE GEÏLLUSTREERDE PERS BV Camera: PENTAX 6x7 Film: FUJI RDP Concept & Styling: MATTHIAS VRIENS Country: NETHERLANDS ■ Shoes and furniture of local Dutch artists, photographed for *Avenue* magazine. ● Schuhe, photographiert mit Möbeln von holländischen Designern für die Zeitschrift *Avenue*. ▲ Chaussures et meubles de designers hollandais, photographiés pour le magazine *Avenue*.

PAGE 23 Photographer: ENRIQUE BADULESCU Representative: GIOVANNI TESTINO Publisher/Client: *VOGUE PARIS*/CONDÉ NAST Camera: KONICA PRESS Film: FUJI FP100 Art Director: DONALD SCHNEIDER Designer: YOHJI YAMAMOTO Country: FRA ■ Editorial photograph taken for *Vogue Paris*. ● Redaktionelle Aufnahme für *Vogue Paris*. ▲ Photo rédactionnelle pour *Vogue Paris*.

PAGE 24 Photographer: ENRIQUE BADULESCU Representative: MICHELE FILOMENO Publisher/Client: *VOGUE PARIS*/CONDÉ NAST Camera: PENTAX POLAROID BACK Film: FUJI FP100 Art Director: DONALD SCHNEIDER Fashion Designer: THIERRY MUGLER Country: FRA ■ Fashion photograph taken for *Vogue Paris*. ● Modeaufnahme für *Vogue Paris*. ▲ Photo de mode publiée dans *Vogue Paris*.

PAGE 25 Photographer: SATOSHI SAIKUSA Representative: ERIC BLANPIED Publisher/Client: *VOGUE ITALIA*/EDIZIONI CONDÉ NAST S.P.A. Art Director: LUCA STOPPINI Country: ITALY ■ Fashion photograph that appeared in *Vogue Italia*. ● Diese Modeaufnahme stammt aus der italienischen *Vogue*. ▲ Photo de mode publiée dans l'édition italienne *Vogue*.

PAGES 26, 27 Photographer: KENJI TOMA Representative: MICHAEL ASH Client/Agency: NEIMAN MARCUS ADVERTISING Camera: HORSEMAN 4x5" Film: KODAK VHC Art Director: PEGGY BENNETT Country: USA ■ Fashion accessories. ● Mode-Accessoires ▲ Accessoires mode.

PAGE 28 Photographer: KENJI TOMA Representative: MICHAEL ASH Client: BLOOMINGDALE'S Camera: DEARDORF 8x10 Film: KODAK EPP Art Director: KRISTI KROENER Country: USA ■ "Playing with colors and form." Fashion photograph for Bloomingdale's. ● «Spiel mit Farbe und Form.» Modeaufnahme für das Kaufhaus Bloomingdale's. ▲ «Jeu de formes et de couleurs». Photo de mode pour le magasin Bloomingdale's.

PAGE 29 Photographer: KENJI TOMA Representative: MICHAEL ASH Publisher: *MADEMOISELLE* Camera: HORSEMAN 4x5 Film: KODAK EPP Art Director: CINDY SEARIGHT Country: USA ■ "Playing with colors again." Fashion photograph published in *Mademoiselle*. ● «Man spielt wieder mit Farben.» Modeaufnahme für die Zeitschrift *Mademoiselle*. ▲ «La couleur se fait ludique.» Photo de mode pour le magazine *Mademoiselle*.

PAGE 30 Photographer: RODNEY SMITH Representative: MICHAEL ASH Publisher: *MIRABELLA* Camera: HASSELBLAD Films: KODAK TRI-X/KODAK PLUS-X FASHION DIRECTOR: HEIDI BARON Designer: MARCOS GAGO Country: USA ■ Swimwear by Calvin Klein. The series was produced in two days at various Long Island estates. ● Bademode von Calvin Klein. Die Serie wurde an zwei Tagen auf verschiedenen Anwesen von Long Island aufgenommen. ▲ Maillots de bain Calvin Klein. Cette série a été réalisée en deux jours, dans différentes propriétés de Long Island.

PAGE 31 Photographer: STEVEN MEISEL Representative: JIM MOFFAT/ART + COMMERCE Publisher/Client: *VOGUE*/THE CONDÉ NAST PUBLICATION INC. Art Director: RAUL MARTINEZ Fashion Designer: GALLIANO Country: USA ■ "A dress fit for a '30s Hollywood star"—Linda Evangelista photographed for a fashion feature in *Vogue*. ● «Ein Kleid, das einem Hollywood Star der 30er Jahre angemessen wäre.» Modeaufnahme mit Linda Evangelista für die amerikanische *Vogue*. ▲ «Robe dessinée à l'image d'une star hollywoodienne des années 30». Photo de Linda Evangelista pour l'édition américaine de *Vogue*.

PAGE 32 Photographer: NICK KNIGHT Representative: CHARLOTTE WHEELER Publisher/Client: *VOGUE*/THE CONDÉ NAST PUBLICATION INC. Camera: MAMIYA RZ Film: EKTACHROME 200 Exposure: F22/400 Art Director: RAUL MARTINEZ Fashion Designer: CHANEL Country: USA ■ "Techno Vision." Linda Evangelista wears a bra made of metallic leather, adding a modern touch to the traditional ski suit. The image originally appeared in a fashion feature in AmericanVogue. ● «Techno-Look.» Linda Evangelista trägt einen BH aus Leder, der dem klassischen Ski-Anzug einen modernen Touch gibt. Die Aufnahme gehört zu einem Modebeitrag in der amerikanischen *Vogue*. ▲ Le look techno. Linda Evangelista porte un soutien-gorge en cuir qui confère une touche techno à l'ensemble de ski classique. Cette photo fut publiée dans l'édition américaine de *Vogue*.

PAGE 33 Photographer: GILES HANCOCK Representative: COREY GRAHAM Camera: CAMBO 4x5" Film: KODAK VPS Exposure: F22/MULTIPLE, TUNGSTEN & FLASH Art Director/Designer: GILES HANCOCK Country: USA ■ This image was inspired by the "Spirit of Ecstasy" figurehead on Rolls Royce automobiles and Maxfield Parrish's style of painting. It is actually made up of different elements—the model, the platform, and the painted background—and was composed on the computer. The shot was originally executed in color and then converted to black-and-white on the computer. With reference to old-style movie effects and techniques, the image was meant to look stylized and surreal. It was used in the photographer's self-promotion mailer. ● Dieses Bild wurde von der Rolls-Royce-Figur «Spirit of Ecstasy» und dem Malstil von Maxfield Parrish inspiriert. Es besteht eigentlich aus verschiedenen Elementen – dem Modell selbst, der Aufmachung des Modells, der Plattform und dem gemalten Hintergrund –, die im Computer zusammengefügt wurden. Die Aufnahme wurde in Farbe gemacht und dann im Computer in Schwarzweiss umgewandelt. Als Anspielung auf Effekte und Techniken alter Filme sollte das Bild stilisiert und surreal wirken. Der Photograph verwendete es als Eigenwerbung. ▲ Image inspirée de la célèbre figure de proue des Rolls-Royce, «The Spirit of Ecstasy», et du style propre au peintre Maxfield Parrish. Les divers éléments – le modèle, l'estrade et le fond peint – ont été réalisés sur ordinateur. La photo originale, en couleur, a également été retravaillée sur ordinateur et transformée en image noir et blanc. Pour évoquer les effets et les techniques des anciens films, l'image devait être stylisée et surréaliste. Le photographe l'a utilisée pour un mailing autopromotionnel.

PAGE 34 Photographer: ELLEN VON UNWERTH Representative: ART + COMMERCE Publisher/Client: *VOGUE*/THE CONDÉ NAST PUBLICATION INC. Art Director: RAUL MARTINEZ Country: USA ■ "Diary of a Spa." Image that originally appeared in a fashion feature of American Vogue. ● «Tagebuch aus einem Mineralbad», diese Aufnahme stammt aus einem Modebeitrag in der amerikanischen *Vogue*. ▲ «Journal d'une source thermale». Photo publiée dans l'édition américaine de *Vogue*.

PAGE 35 Photographer: PETER LINDBERGH Representative: MARION DE BEAUPRÉ PRODUCTIONS Publisher/Client: *HARPER'S BAZAAR*/THE HEARST CORPORATION Country: USA ■ "Let it Rain." Image from a fashion feature in *Harper's Bazaar*. ● «Lass' es regnen» – Aufnahme aus einem Modebeitrag in *Harper's Bazaar*. ▲ «Let it rain». Photo publiée dans *Harper's Bazaar*.

PAGES 36, 37 (top right and bottom left) Photographer: SARAH MOON Representative: BARBARA VON SCHREIBER Publisher: *NEW YORK TIMES MAGAZINE* Camera: POLAROID Film: POLAROID Art Director: JANET FROELICH Designer: CATHY GILMORE-BARNES Stylist: FRANS ANKONE Country: USA ■ "Hidden in the Folds—The Languor of Drapery in the Classical Mode." The way Sasha Robertson moved and held her body created the folds and gave the fabric a life of its own. The blouse is by Comme des Garçons. ● «Verborgen in den Falten – der verführerische Faltenwurf in der klassischen Mode.» Durch ihre Haltung und Bewegungen gab Sasha Robertson dem Stoff ein eigenes Leben. Die Bluse ist von Comme des Garçons. ▲ «Les drapés de charme de la mode classique». Le tissu prend vie au gré des ondulations imprimées par le corps de Sasha Robertson. Elle porte une blouse Comme des Garçons.

PAGE 37 (top left and bottom right) Photographer: SARAH MOON Representative: BARBARA VON SCHREIBER Publisher: *NEW YORK TIMES MAGAZINE* Camera: POLAROID Film: POLAROID Art Director: JANET FROELICH Designer: LISA NAFTOLIN Stylist: FRANS ANKONE Country: USA ■ Top left and bottom right: "Scotland by the Yard—The Case for Tartan Plaid." The photographer's response to the tartan theme is to use very strong colored backgrounds to complement the color of the clothes. Top right and bottom left: images from a series on the effect of folds (see also page 36). ● Oben links und unten rechts: «Schottland per Yard – Ein Fall für Schottenstoffe.» Die Photographin interpretierte das Thema «Schottenstoffe» durch starke Farben im Hintergrund als Ergänzung der Farben des Stoffes. Oben rechts und unten links: Diese Bilder gehören zu der Studie des klassischen Faltenwurfes (siehe auch Seite 36). ▲ En haut à gauche et en bas à droite: «L'Ecosse, vue par le Yard – Le mystère des tartans». La photographe a interprété le thème tartan en choisissant un fond aux couleurs vives en harmonie avec les tissus. En haut à droite et en bas à gauche: images tirées de l'étude sur les drapés classiques (voir également en page 36).

PAGE 38 Photographer: RINEKE DIJKSTRA Representative: HEDY VAN ERP Publisher/Client: *AVENUE*/DE GEÏLLUSTREERDE PERS BV Camera: WISTA 4x5 Film: KODAK VPS Art Director: HANS VAN BLOMMESTEIN Country: NETHERLANDS ■ The assignment of *Avenue* magazine had simply been to photograph the dress. The photographer chose to do it on the beach, and then the dog passed by and she asked him to pose for her. ● Der Auftrag der Zeitschrift *Avenue* lautete schlicht, das Kleid zu photographieren. Die Photographin beschloss, dies am Strand zu tun. Zufällig kam ein Hund vorbei, und sie bat ihn, für sie zu posieren. ▲ Le mandat du magazine *Avenue* était simplement de photographier la robe. La photographe choisit d'exécuter son travail à la plage, et, lorsqu'un chien vint à passer, elle lui demanda de poser.

PAGE 39 Photographer: MICHEL COMTE Representative: LUKAS ALBERS Client: ARMANI EXCHANGE/GIORGIO ARMANI Art Directors: ANDREA D'AQUINO, MARTY WEISS Agency: WEISS, WHITTEN, STAGLIANO Country: USA ■ "A reminder that dressing casually can still be considered dressing elegantly." Image used on the cover of A/X, Armani Exchange, that featured a new spring line. ● «Eine Erinnerung daran, dass sich bequem kleiden noch immer bedeuten kann, sich elegant zu kleiden.» Die Aufnahme wurde für den Umschlag eines A/X (Armani Exchange) Katalogs verwendet, in dem Frühjahrsmode vorgestellt wurde. ▲ «Petit clin d'œil pour se rappeler que l'on peut aimer le confort sans sacrifier à l'élégance.» Cette image illustra la couverture d'un catalogue A/X (Armani Exchange) consacré à la nouvelle mode de printemps.

PAGE 40 Photographer: JUERGEN TELLER Representative: Z PHOTOGRAPHIC Publisher/Client: *VOGUE*/THE CONDÉ NAST PUBLICATION INC. Country: USA ■ "Red Hot." A fresh twist on the season's little slip dress. This image originally appeared in American *Vogue*. ● Heisses Rot, eine frische Variante der Hemdkleider der Saison. Das Bild erschien in der amerikanischen *Vogue*. ▲ En rouge flamboyant, une variante séduisante des robes chemise de la saison. Photo publiée dans l'édition américaine de *Vogue*.

PAGE 41 (right) Photographer: FRIDHELM VOLK Client: BRANDT-ECCO AG Camera: CONTAX Country: GERMANY ■ Image used as an illustration in the annual report of a fashion company. ● Die Aufnahme diente als Illustration des Jahresberichts eines Modeherstellers. ▲ Cette photo illustre le rapport annuel d'une maison de couture.

PAGE 42 Photographer: RACHEL JEROME Camera: MAMIYA 6x7 Film: KODAK T-MAX 100 Art Director: B FERRARO Country: USA ■ One from a series on models in black dresses. ● Eine von mehreren Aufnahmen von Modellen in schwarzen Kleidern. ▲ Photo tirée d'une série sur des mannequins, tout de noir vêtus.

PAGE 43 Photographer: KLAUS MITTELDORF Representative: AGNES SCHWENZEL Publisher: *MADAME* Camera: PENTAX 6x7 Film: EKTACHROME EPP Exposure: F11/125 Country: BRASIL ■ The haircut of the model, the cut of the swimsuit, and the landscape work together to create a strong graphic image. ● Bademode, auf sehr graphische Art dargestellt: der Haarschnitt des Modells, der Schnitt des Badeanzugs und die Landschaft, alle Elemente entsprachen ideal der gewünschten graphischen Wirkung. ▲ Maillot de bain présenté de manière très graphique: la coupe de cheveux du modèle, la coupe du maillot et le paysage se complètent idéalement pour créer l'effet graphique recherché.

PAGE 44 Photographer: ALDO FALLAI Representative: STUDIO REPOSSI S.R.L. Client: GIORGIO ARMANI SPA Art Director: ROSANNA ARMANI Agency: ARMANI PRESS & PUBLIC RELATIONS STUDIO S.R.L. Country: ITALY ■ Image used in a catalog for Italian fashion designer Giorgio Armani. ● Das Bild wurde in einem Katalog des italienischen Modeschöpfers Giorgio Armani verwendet. ▲ Photo publiée dans un catalogue Armani.

PAGE 45 Photographer: ARTHUR ELGORT Representative: MARIANNE HOUTENBOS Publisher/Client: *VOGUE*/THE CONDÉ NAST PUBLICATION INC. Fashion Editor: BRANA WOLF Country: USA ■ Shalom Harlow, photographed in natural light in the train station lobby of Southampton, Long Island, for a fashion feature in *Vogue*. ● Das Modell Shalom Harlow, aufgenommen bei natürlichem Licht im Wartesaal des Bahnhofs von Southampton, Long Island, für einen Modebeitrag in der amerikanischen *Vogue*. ▲ Le mannequin Shalom Harlow, photographié à la lumière du jour dans la salle d'attente de la gare de Southampton, Long Island, pour l'édition américaine de *Vogue*.

PAGE 46 Photographer: RODNEY SMITH Representative: MICHAEL ASH Publisher: *W MAGAZINE* Camera: FUJICA 6x7 Films: KODAK TRI-X, KODAK PLUS-X Creative Director: DENNIS FREEDMAN Fashion Editor: ROBERT BRYAN Country: USA ■ The photographer went to Hancock, a Shaker village in Massachusetts, for this fashion show. Shown is a cotton shirt by Perry Ellis and a hat by Borsalino. ● Der Photograph wählte das Shaker-Dorf Hancock in Massachusetts als Ort für seine Modeaufnahmen. Gezeigt ist ein Baumwollhemd von Perry Ellis und ein Borsalino. ▲ Pour réaliser ses photos de mode, le photographe choisit de se rendre à Shaker village Hancock dans le Massachusetts. Chemise en coton Perry Ellis et chapeau Borsalino.

PAGE 47 Photographer: ELLEN VON UNWERTH Representative: ART + COMMERCE Publisher/Client: *VOGUE*/THE CONDÉ NAST PUBLICATION INC. Art Director: RAUL MARTINEZ Country: USA ■ The timeless appeal of classic Greek-style gowns was the theme of a fashion feature in American *Vogue*. ● Die zeitlose Schönheit von Kleidern im griechischen Stil war das Thema eines Modebeitrags in der amerikanischen *Vogue*. ▲ La beauté intemporelle des vêtements inspirés de la Grèce antique fit l'objet d'un article dans l'édition américaine de *Vogue*.

PAGE 48 Photographer: DOMINIQUE DDIEULOT Representative: ROUCHON & Co. Publisher/Client: *AVENUE*/DE GEÏLLUSTREERDE PERS BV Camera: PENTAX SUPER A Film: KODAK EKTACHROME EES 800/1600 Exposure: F5.6/60 Art Director: FRANS ANKONE Fashion Designer: JEAN PAUL GAULTIER Country: NETHERLANDS ■ The photographer considered her subject as a sculpture: the body served as a support for the garments. The photographer took the shots as she circled around the still model, focusing on the curves, the movement of the fabrics, the graphic side of the body lines. She worked in daylight with a mandarine RC 80 800 W filter. ● Die Photographin behandelte ihr Modell wie eine Skulptur: der Körper diente als Stütze für Kleider, und sie war es, die sich um das Modell herum bewegte, nachdem dieses einmal die gewünschte Haltung eingenommen hatte. Sie konzentrierte sich auf die Formen, die Bewegungen des Stoffes, auf die graphische Wirkung der Körperformen. Dabei arbeitete die Photographin bei Tageslicht mit einem Mandarin-RC 80-800-W-Filter. ▲ La photographe transforma son modèle en sculpture: le corps sert de support aux vêtements et, une fois la position voulue trouvée, c'est elle qui évolua autour du mannequin. Elle s'attacha à capter le mouvement des tissus et le côté graphique des lignes du corps. Elle travailla pour ce faire avec la lumière du jour et un filtre RC 80 800 W mandarine.

PAGE 49 Photographer: NADAV KANDER Representative: STOCKLAND MARTEL Client: GAP BOOTS USA Art Director: KEVIN REDMAN Agency: GAP ADVERTISING Country: USA ■ Advertising shot of mannequin wearing GAP boots. ● Mannequin in GAP-Stiefeln, aufgenommen für eine Anzeige. ▲ Mannequin chaussé de bottes GAP, photographié pour une publicité.

PAGE 50 Photographer: MARIO TESTINO Representatives: GIOVANNI TESTINO, USA, MICHELE FILOMENO, EUROPE Publisher/Client: HARPER'S BAZAAR/THE HEARST CORPORATION Country: USA ■ Jean-Paul Goude, the imagemaker, in action on a rooftop set that he constructed to photograph Karen Parks as "Kareen of Seoul." The velvet gown is by French costume designer Marie Beltrami. ● Der berühmte Werbemann Jean-Paul Goude in Aktion auf einem Dach, wo er eine Konstruktion aufbaute, um Karen Parks als «Kareen of Seoul» photographieren zu lassen. Das Samtkleid ist von der Kostümbildnerin Marie Beltrami. ▲ Jean-Paul Goude, le célèbre publiciste, en action sur un toit où il édifia une construction pour photographier Karen Parks simulant «Kareen of Seoul». La robe de velours a été créée par la costumière Marie Beltrami.

PAGE 51 Photographer: STEVEN MEISEL Representative: JIM MOFFAT/ART + COMMERCE Publisher: VOGUE ITALIA/EDIZIONI CONDÉ NAST S.P.A. Country: ITALY ■ Linda Evangelista photographed for a fashion feature in Vogue Italia. ● Modeaufnahme mit Linda Evangelista für die italienische Vogue. ▲ Photo de Linda Evangelista publiée dans Vogue Italie.

PAGES 52, 53 Photographer: HERB RITTS Representative: VISAGES Publisher/Client: VOGUE/THE CONDÉ NAST PUBLICATION INC. Country: USA ■ "Beauty's New Wave." The theme of these images is the cosmetic industry's discovery of the ocean. ● «Die neue Welle für die Schönheit», das Thema dieser Aufnahmen ist die neue Vorliebe der Kosmetikindustrie für das Meer. ▲ «La Beauté nouvelle vague». Ces images illustrent le nouvel amour porté par l'industrie des cosmétiques à la mer et à ses bienfaits.

PAGE 54 Photographer: THOMAS SCHENK Publisher/Client: AVENUE/DE GEÏLLUSTREERDE PERS BV Camera: PENTAX 6X7 Film: FUJI RDP Concept & Styling: MATTHIAS VRIENS Country: NETHERLANDS ■ Karl Lagerfeld's plastic-lined boot just asked for the sushi fish. ● Karl Lagerfelds Stiefel mit dem Plastiküberzug schien geradezu nach einem Sushi-Fisch zu verlangen. ▲ Botte Karl Lagerfeld entourée d'un plastique et semblant faire un pied de nez à un poisson.

PAGE 55 Photographer: JAVIER VALLHONRAT Representative: MICHELE FILOMENO Publisher/Client: VOGUE PARIS/CONDÉ NAST Country: FRANCE ■ Fashion shot for French Vogue. ● Modeaufnahme für die französische Vogue. ▲ Photo publiée dans Vogue.

PAGE 56 Photographer: MARIO TESTINO Representatives: GIOVANNI TESTINO, USA, MICHELE FILOMENO, EUROPE Publisher/Client: HARPER'S BAZAAR/THE HEARST CORPORATION Country: USA ■ "Red is a Girl's Best Friend." Diana Vreeland is wearing a long velour T-shirt dress by Isaac Mizrahi. ● «Rot ist eines Mädchens bester Freund». Diana Vreeland trägt ein langes T-Shirt-Kleid aus Samt von Isaac Mizrahi. ▲ «Le rouge est le meilleur allié des filles». Diana Vreeland est vêtue d'une longue robe tee-shirt en velours de Isaac Mizrahi.

PAGE 57 Photographer: BOB FRAME Representative: PROOF Client: BLOOMINGDALE'S Camera: PENTAX 6X7 Film: KODAK TRI-X Art Director: PAUL NISKI Designer: STUDIO N DESIGN Country: USA ■ "Intimacies." Image used for a catalog cover for Bloomingdale's department store. The delicate nature of the lingerie is reinforced by the wire hanger. ● Diese Aufnahme diente als Umschlag eines Katalogs mit Dessous des Kaufhauses Bloomingdale's. Der Drahtbügel unterstreicht die Zartheit der Wäsche. ▲ Cette photo

illustra la page de couverture d'un catalogue de sous-vêtements féminins Bloomingdale's. Le cintre métallique contraste avec la délicatesse de la lingerie.

PAGE 58 Photographer: NADAV KANDER Representative: STOCKLAND MARTEL Client: KARASTAN CARPETS Camera: POLAROID 8x10" Art Director: BOB RANEW Agency: MCKINNEY & SILVER Country: USA ■ The client, a manufacturer of carpets and rugs, wanted their product to look like a fashion item rather than a commodity. The photographer came up with this fine art approach, making it look like a museum piece. ● Der Kunde, ein Teppichhersteller, wollte seine Ware als Modeartikel und nicht als Gebrauchsgegenstand dargestellt sehen. Die Lösung: den Teppich auf künstlerische Art wie ein Museumsstück zu photographieren. ▲ Le client, un fabricant de tapis, voulait que son produit ressemble à un article de mode plutôt qu'à un objet utilitaire. La solution: photographier le tapis de manière artistique afin qu'il prenne des allures de pièce de musée.

PAGE 59 Photographer: NADAV KANDER Representative: STOCKLAND MARTEL Client: NIKE Art Director: WARREN EAKINS Agency: WIEDEN & KENNEDY, AMSTERDAM Country: USA ■ Advertising shot for Nike. ● Werbeaufnahme für Nike. ▲ Publicité pour Nike.

PAGES 70, 72 Photographer: GERD AUMEIER Client: RESTEK ELECTRONIK PRODUKTS GMBH Camera: SINAR P 13x18 Film: KODAK EPP 100 Country: GERMANY ■ Images of flowers used within a catalog for high-end music equipment. The photographer looked for a solution that would both harmonize with and contrast to the pure design of the products. For each image he combined parts of two different dried plants/flowers, which he shot on a white ground lighted from below. Light from the side was supplied through Hosemaster Lightpainting. ● Der Auftrag verlangte Blumenaufnahmen für einen Katalog für anspruchsvolle Musikanlagen. Der Photograph suchte nach einer Lösung, die einerseits einen Kontrapunkt zum Design der Geräte setzte, andererseits zu den Produkten passte. Für jede Aufnahme kombinierte er Teile von zwei verschiedenen Pflanzen/Blumen, die auf weissem Untergrund mit Unterlicht angeordnet und mit Seitenlicht (Hosemaster Lightpainting) aufgenommen wurden. ▲ Il s'agissait de réaliser des photos de fleurs pour illustrer un catalogue d'installations stéréo haut de gamme. Le photographe recherche une solution à même de fournir un contrepoint au côté design des appareils tout en étant adaptée aux produits. Il combina ainsi pour chaque prise de vue des parties de fleurs ou de plantes différentes qu'il photographia sur un fond blanc éclairé par dessous et sur les côtés (Hosemaster Lightpainting).

PAGE 73 Photographers: ANDREA GENTL, MARTY HYERS Publisher: CONDÉ NAST TRAVELER Camera: DEARDORF 8x10" Film: POLAROID Art Director: MICHELLE BUFFINGTON Country: USA ■ A still life from the tea salon Emporium below the Guggenheim Museum in Soho, an assignment for the magazine Condé Nast Traveler. ● Stilleben aus der Teestube unterhalb des Guggenheim-Museums in Soho, ein Auftrag einer Reisezeitschrift. ▲ Nature morte prise dans le salon de thé «Emporium», situé en dessous du musée Guggenheim à Soho. Cette photo a été réalisée pour un magazine de voyages.

PAGE 74 Photographer: LISA SPINDLER Representative: MICHAEL ASH Camera: NIKON F3 Film: KODAK T-MAX 100 Country: USA ■ A personal study of the back of an antherium leaf. ● Persönliche Studie der Rückseite eines Anthurium-Blattes. ▲ Etude du dessous d'une feuille.

PAGE 75 Photographer: MARK LAITA Camera: FATIF 8x10" Film: KODAK T-MAX 100 Country: USA ■ Part of a series on shapes and textures found in nature. The black-and-white print was toned in selenium and gold to achieve its saturated color. ● Diese Aufnahme ist Teil einer Serie über Formen und Texturen in der Natur. Um die gewünschte satte Farbtönung zu erreichen, wurde der Schwarzweiss-Abzug mit Selenium- und Goldtönungen behandelt. ▲ Image extraite d'une série sur les formes et les matières dans la nature. Pour obtenir ces tons chauds, le tirage noir et blanc a été viré au sélénium et à l'or.

PAGE 76 Photographer: IMRE GABOR ECK Camera: LINHOF KARDAN 4x5" Film: AGFAPAN 100 Exposure: FLASH Country: HUNGARY ■ A personal study on the beauty of old tools. ● Persönliche Studie der Schönheit alter Werkzeuge. ▲ Etude sur des outils.

PAGE 77 Photographer: ANDRÉ BARANOWSKI Client: GOLDEN CAPRICORN PUBLICATION Camera: MAMIYA RZ 67 Film: FUJI VELVIA Art Director: ANDRÉ BARANOWSKI Country:

USA ■ One of a series of images marked by simplicity, beauty, and grace of the composition. ● Ein Bild aus einer Serie, die sich durch Schlichtheit, Schönheit und Anmut der Komposition auszeichnet. ▲ Image extraite d'une série qui se distingue par la simplicité, la beauté et la grâce de la composition.

PAGES 78, 79 Photographer: SIGURD KRANENDONK Representative: PIM THOMASSEN Publisher/Client: *AVENUE*/DE GEÏLLUSTREERDE PERS BV Camera: CAMBO 13x18 Film: FUJI VELVIA 13x18 Exposure: F45 Art Director: HANS VAN BLOMMESTEIN Country: NETHER-LANDS ■ Image inspired by a 17th-century Dutch still-life painting. Broncolor flash equipment was used to imitate the quality of natural daylight typical of that period. ● Das Bild entstand nach dem Vorbild eines Stillebens der holländischen Schule aus dem 17. Jahrhundert. Das für die Zeit typische Tageslicht wurde durch Broncolor-Blitz erreicht. ▲ Photo inspirée d'une nature morte hollandaise du 17e siècle. La lumière typique du style de l'époque a été obtenue grâce à un flash Broncolor.

PAGE 80 Photographer: RICARDO DE VICQ DE CUMPTICH Camera: SINAR P Film: KODAK EKTACHROME 4x5" Exposure: F32.5 Designer: RICARDO DE VICQ DE CUMPTICH Country: BRAZIL ■ Image from a personal series on the beauty of flowers. The desired effect was obtained through multiple exposures and light painting. ● Das Bild gehört zu einer Serie über die Schönheit von Blumen. Der gewünschte Effekt wurde durch Mehrfachbelichtung und Lightpainting erreicht. ▲ Image extraite d'une série mettant en exergue la beauté des fleurs. L'effet désiré a été obtenu par exposition multiple et lightpainting.

PAGES 81, 82 Photographer: CRAIG CUTLER Camera: TOYO 4x5" Film: KODAK T-MAX Stylist: ANITA CALERO Country: USA ■ Macro shots of ordinary metal objects on metal plates. Limited focus was achieved by disregarding the conventional techniques of shooting with a view camera (swings and tilts). A lens from the late 1940s helped convey an unpolished feeling. ● Makro-Aufnahmen von gewöhnlichen Metallgegenständen auf Metallplatten. Um die begrenzte Schärfentiefe zu erreichen, wurden die konventionellen Einstellungstechniken der Fachkamera (Schwenken und Verschieben) absichtlich nicht genutzt. Ein Objektiv aus den späten vierziger Jahren verstärkte den «ungeschliffenen» Eindruck. ▲ Macrophotos d'objets métalliques courants posés sur des plaques en métal. La profondeur de champ limitée a été obtenue en bafouant toutes les principes de règlage avec une chambre professionnelle (basculer et décentrement). Le côté «brut» a été obtenu grâce à un objectif datant de la fin des années quarante.

PAGE 83 Photographer: KATHRYN KLEINMAN Client: COLLINS PUBLISHERS Camera: NIKON FM Film: 3M SCOTCH 1000 Exposure: F8/250 Art Directors: KATHRYN KLEINMAN, MICHAELE THUNEN Designer: JENNIFER BARRY Country: USA ■ "Icelandic Poppies on Leaves." This image is taken from a book entitled *Souvenirs—Gifts from the Garden*, a collection of natural-light photographs showing the beauty found in nature throughout the seasons. ● «Mohnknospen» auf Blättern». Das Bild stammt aus dem Buch *Souvenirs – Gifts from the Garden*, eine Sammlung von Bildern, die, bei Tageslicht aufgenommen, die Schönheit der Natur in allen Jahreszeiten zeigen. ▲ «Bourgeons de pavot sur des feuilles.» Photo extraite d'un livre intitulé *Souvenirs – Gifts from the Garden*, une collection d'images prise à la lumière du jour et illustrant la beauté de la nature à travers les saisons.

PAGE 84 Photographers: WALTER COLLEY/KAMPER SPROUSE COLLEY Representative: GLYNIS VALENTI Camera: SINAR Film: KODAK EKTACHROME PLUS Exposure: F9/2 SEC. Art Director: DEREK SNAPE Country: USA ■ In order to obtain a soft look, a mix of daylight strobes and Tungsten lighting was used while the shutter was open long enough to capture the shaking movement. ● Um eine sanfte Stimmung zu erzeugen, wurde eine Mischung von Blitz und Kunstlichtlicht benutzt. Zudem war die Verschlusszeit lang genug, um das Bild leicht zu verwackeln. ▲ Pour créer une atmosphère romantique, le photographe recourt à la lumière du tungstène et à un éclairage stroboscopique tandis que la vitesse d'obturateur lui permet d'obtenir un léger flou.

PAGE 85 Photographer: ROBERT TARDIO Representative: COLEEN MCKAY Camera: 4x5 SINAR P2 Film: KODAK PLUS X Art Director: ROBERT TARDIO Country: USA ■ The image is part of a series of still life images created to show the drama of one object. ● Das Bild gehört zu einer Serie von Stilleben, bei denen es dem Photographen um die Dramatik einzelner Objekte geht. ▲ Cette photo fait partie d'une série de natures mortes. Pour le photographe, il s'agissait de faire ressortir l'aspect dramatique d'objets pris individuellement.

PAGE 86 Photographer: JENNY LYNN Representative: JOHN HOPKINS Camera: OLYMPUS OM-1 Film: KODAK LUMIERE 100 Exposures: F5.6/60, F8/60 Country: USA ■ "The Butterfly and the Mask" from a series entitled "Doubles," an exploration of the double exposure. As the Olympus OM-1 is not designed to make double exposures, the results are part plan and part chance, which give the image a mysterious life of its own. ● «Der Schmetterling und die Maske» gehört zu einer Serie, in der die Photographin mit Doppelbelichtungen experimentierte. Da die Olympus-OM-l-Kamera nicht für Doppelbelichtungen gemacht wurde, sind die Ergebnisse halb Planung halb Zufall, was den Bildern eine geheimnisvolle Eigenständigkeit gibt. ▲ «Le papillon et le masque». Photo extraite d'une série qui permit à la photographe de travailler la surimpression. Comme son appareil Olympus OM-1 n'est pas fait pour ce type de photos, le résultat est en partie voulu et en partie le fruit du hasard, ce qui confère aux images un côté mystérieux.

PAGE 87 Photographer: JENNIFER BAUMANN Camera: CONTAX RTS Film: AGFACHROME 1000 Exposure: F11/1/15 sec. Art Director: JENNIFER BAUMANN Country: USA ■ This image is part of a personal project exploring the depth of color in colorlessness. ● Dieses Bild gehört zu einem Projekt der Photographin, bei dem sie sich mit der Tiefe der Farbe in Farblosigkeit befasst. ▲ Cette image fait partie d'une étude de l'artiste sur la profondeur des couleurs dans l'absence de couleurs.

PAGE 88 Photographer: LIZZIE HIMMEL Representative: PROOF Publisher: *NEW YORK TIMES MAGAZINE* Art Director: JANET FROELICH Designer: PETRA MERCKER Country: USA ■ Samples of the multicolored Mandan Bride, a traditionally pollinated field corn that is native to American soil. The photo served as an opener to an article entitled "The Seed Conspiracy," dealing with the question of hybrids. ● «Mandan Bride», ein traditionelles Feldkorn aus Nordamerika, das sich durch Bestäubung vermehrt. Die Aufnahme diente als Aufmacher für einen Artikel mit dem Titel «Die Samen-Verschwörung» über Hybriden und die Folgen für die Natur. ▲ Echantillons de graines «Mandan Bride», variété cultivée en Amérique du Nord qui se reproduit par pollinisation. Cette photo illustrait un article intitulé «La conspiration des semences» sur le thème des hybrides.

PAGE 90 Photographer: SIGURD KRANENDONK Representative: PIM THOMASSEN Publisher/Client: *AVENUE*/DE GEÏLLUSTREERDE PERS BV Camera: CAMBO 13x18 Film: FUJI VELVIA Exposure: F64 Art Director: HANS VAN BLOMMESTEIN Country: NETHERLANDS ■ "Still Life with Pig's Head," a photograph inspired by a 17th-century Dutch still-life painting. To imitate the quality of natural daylight typical of that period, the photographer used Broncolor flash equipment. ● «Stilleben mit Schweinskopf», eine Aufnahme nach einem Stilleben der holländischen Schule aus dem 17. Jahrhundert. Um die für die Zeit typische Tageslichtqualität zu erreichen, verwendete der Photograph Broncolor-Blitzlicht. ▲ «Nature morte avec tête de porc», un cliché inspiré d'une nature morte de l'Ecole hollandaise du 17e siècle. Pour obtenir la lumière caractéristique des œuvres de l'époque, le photographe a utilisé un flash Broncolor.

PAGE 91 (top) Photographer: JOYCE OUDKERK POOL Representative: CATHRYN BLUM Camera: NIKON FE2 Film: POLACHROM Exposure: F2.8/1/15 sec. Country: USA ■ Example from a fruit series done with Polaroid's Polachrom 35mm film, which produces a grainy look in the images, especially when blown up. It takes only two minutes to develop the film in an instant processing machine. It is then duped in a lab to a larger format. ● Beispiel aus einer Serie von Stilleben mit Früchten, aufgenommen mit Polachrom-35mm-Film von Polaroid, mit dem sich eine bestimmte Körnigkeit der Bilder erreichen lässt. Dank einem Sofortentwicklungsgerät erhält man das Ergebnis in nur zwei Minuten. Später wird vergrössert, damit die Körnigkeit zum Tragen kommt. ▲ Exemple tiré d'une série de natures mortes représentant des fruits, photographié avec un film Polaroid Polachrom de 35mm. Après le développement instantané qui ne dure que deux minutes, l'image a été agrandie pour souligner la qualité de grain spéciale propre à ce film.

PAGE 91 (bottom) Photographer: DEBORAH JONES Representative: NORMAN MASLOV Client: COLLINS PUBLISHERS Camera: NIKON F3 Creative Director: JENNIFER BARRY Designer: KARI PERIN Country: USA ■ This image was taken for a cookbook showing the beauty and versatility of squash. ● Diese Aufnahme war ein Auftrag für ein Kochbuch über die Schönheit und Vielseitigkeit des Kürbisgemüses. ▲ Image servant à l'illustration d'un livre de cuisine consacré à l'esthétique et aux vertus culinaires du potiron.

PAGE 92 Photographer: ROSANNE OLSON Camera: 4x5" Film: POLAROID 55 Country: USA ■ Example from a pear series taken for a personal Christmas card. ● Aufnahme aus einer

Serie von Stilleben mit Birnen, für eine persönliche Weihnachtskarte der Photographin verwendet. ▲ Image extraite d'une série de natures mortes avec des poires, utilisée par l'artiste pour illustrer une carte de Noël.

PAGE 93 Photographer: SIGURD KRANENDONK Representative: PIM THOMASSEN Publisher/Client: *AVENUE*/DE GEÏLLUSTREERDE PERS BV Camera: CAMBO 4x5" Film: FUJI VELVIA Exposure: F22 Art Director: HANS VAN BLOMMESTEIN Country: NETHERLANDS ■ Two of four "Exclusive Soups" presented in *Avenue* magazine. During the shooting it became very clear that food and color alone, without cutlery, without any styling whatsoever, would serve the purpose best. ● Zwei von vier «exklusiven Suppen», vorgestellt in der Zeitschrift *Avenue*. Es stellte sich bei den Aufnahmen heraus, dass nur die Teller und viel Farbe ohne jegliches Beiwerk die ideale Lösung der Aufgabe waren. ▲ Représentation de deux «Soupes exclusives» publiée dans le magazine *Avenue*. Pour obtenir l'effet recherché, l'accent a été mis sur les assiettes et la couleur, tout artifice superflu ayant volontairement été écarté.

PAGES 94, 95 Photographer: JOHAN DE BOER Publisher: *AVENUE*/DE GEÏLLUSTREERDE PERS BV Camera: PENTAX 6x7 Film: FUJI RDP 120 Art Director: RENÉ ABBÜHL Make-Up: MARION VAN OYEN Country: NETHERLANDS ■ The image was used as an opener for a series of fruit mousse recipes in *Avenue* magazine. The Fuji RDP 120 was processed as a C-41 film. To get the correct skin tone, filtering was used during the shooting. ● Diese Aufnahme diente als Aufmacher für Fruchtmousse-Rezepte in *Avenue*. Der Fuji RDP 120 wurde im C-41-Prozess entwickelt. Der gewünschte Hautton wurde mit Filtern während der Aufnahme erreicht. ▲ Cette image servit d'illustration à des recettes de mousses aux fruits présentées dans le magazine *Avenue*. Le Fuji RDP 120 a été développé avec le processus C-41. L'utilisation de filtres a permis d'obtenir la couleur de peau désirée.

PAGE 96 Photographer: ROSANNE OLSON Camera: 4x5" Film: POLAROID 55 Country: USA ■ Example from a series of pear still lives used for a personal Christmas card. ● Beispiel aus einer Reihe von Stilleben mit Birnen für eine persönliche Weihnachtskarte der Photographin. ▲ Image extraite d'une série de natures mortes avec des poires, utilisée par l'artiste pour illustrer une carte de Noël.

PAGE 97 Photographer: JÖRN ZOLONDEK Representative: GABRIELE SPÄTH Camera: SINAR 8x10" Film: FUJI VELVIA Country: GERMANY ■ Example from a series on fruit. The bananas were cut in slices thin enough to allow the light to penetrate and thick enough not to fall apart. ● Beispiel aus einer Serie mit Früchten. Die Bananen wurden in Scheiben geschnitten, die dünn genug waren, um lichtdurchlässig zu sein, dabei aber dick genug, um nicht zu zerfallen. ▲ Exemple d'une série consacrée aux fruits. Les bananes ont été coupées en tranches suffisamment fines pour laisser passer la lumière.

PAGE 98 Photographer: CHRISTIAN VON ALVENSLEBEN Publisher: *ARCHITEKTUR & WOHNEN* Camera: SINAR 4x5" Film: KODAK EPR Exposure: FLASH Art Director: PETER SCHMIDT Designer/Stylist: HELGA VON ALVENSLEBEN Country: GERMANY ■ A series of kitchen accessories photographed for a magazine on architecture and living. The idea was to raise interest in these tools in a humorous way. ● Küchengeräte, photographiert für die Zeitschrift *Architektur & Wohnen*. Die Idee war, auf humorvolle Art das Interesse an diesen Geräten zu wecken. ▲ Ustensiles de cuisine photographiés pour la revue *Architektur & Wohnen*. L'objectif était de les mettre en valeur de manière humoristique.

PAGE 99 Photographer: THOMAS SCHÜPPING Camera: PLAUBEL 9x12 Film: EKTACHROME EPN Country: GERMANY ■ A still life in the style of the old Dutch masters. In order to obtain the impression of natural light, the fruit were lit through a spot. ● Stilleben im Stil der alten holländischen Meister. Um das Licht natürlich wirken zu lassen, wurden die Früchte mit einem Spot beleuchtet. ▲ Une nature morte dans le style des vieux maîtres hollandais. Pour obtenir une lumière naturelle, les fruits ont été éclairés par un spot.

PAGE 100 Photographer: LUDOVIC MOULIN Country: USA ■ Portrait from a series of personal studies. ● Porträt aus einer Reihe persönlicher Studien. ▲ Portrait extrait d'une série d'études.

PAGES 102, 103 Photographer: MICHELE CLEMENT Representative: NORMAN MASLOV Client: GUESS?, INC. CAMERAS: MAMIYA RZ-120, NIKON FM2 Film: ILFORD FP4 Exposure: VARIOUS Art Director: CHAD FARMER Agency: LAMBESIS COMMUNICATIONS Country: USA ■ Two images for the Guess? home collection. The campaign were to have a European feel

using a loose, editorial approach that would be accessible to all types of people. In most of the images the model's face does not show as she was to represent everybody. ● Zwei Bilder für die Guess?-Wäschekollektion. Die Werbekampagne sollte europäisch wirken und durch die lockere, redaktionell anmutende Darstellung jedermann ansprechen. Die meisten der Aufnahmen zeigen das Gesicht des Modells nicht, weil mit ihr kein bestimmter Typ, sondern alle gemeint sind. ▲ Images utilisées pour une ligne de sous-vêtements Guess?. La campagne devait présenter un caractère européen et s'adresser à un vaste public par une approche rédactionnelle décontractée et attractive. Sur la plupart des images, la tête du mannequin a volontairement été tronquée afin que n'importe quelle femme puisse s'identifier avec le modèle.

PAGE 104 Photographer: BARBARA BORDNICK Camera: HASSELBLAD WITH LEAF DIGITAL BACK Art Director: BARBARA BORDNICK Country: USA ■ "Waiting/Male Nude," from a series on ballet dancers, reproduced as Iris prints. ● «Warten/Männlicher Akt.» Das Bild gehört zu einer Studie über Ballettänzer. Die Aufnahme wurde mit einem Iris-Belichter abgezogen. ▲ «L'attente/Nu masculin». Image extraite d'une série consacrée aux danseurs d'opéra.

PAGES 105, 106 Photographer: RON BAMBRIDGE Representative: JENNY UNGLESS Camera: WISTA 4x5" Film: KODAK EKTACHROME 64 4x5" DAYLIGHT Art Director: RON BAMBRIDGE Country: GREAT BRITAIN ■ These images tell the story of the Watercress line, part of the national railway network in Great Britain that was closed down many years ago for economic reasons. For the past few years, enthusiastic volunteers have made the old steam trains run again and have kept all the stations on the route open, making sure that all the original features are retained and preserved. The people in these images are some of the volunteers. ● Diese Bilder erzählen die Geschichte der Watercress-Eisenbahnlinie. Einst Teil des nationalen Bahnnetzes in Grossbritannien, wurde sie vor vielen Jahren aus wirtschaftlichen Gründen stillgelegt. Vor einigen Jahren brachten Eisenbahnliebhaber die alten Dampfloks wieder zum Laufen und öffneten alle Bahnhöfe an der Strecke, wobei sie darauf achteten, dass der ursprüngliche Zustand der Gebäude erhalten blieb. Diese Aufnahmen zeigen die Freiwilligen bei der Arbeit. ▲ Ces images racontent l'histoire de la ligne de chemin de fer Watercress, jadis part du réseau ferroviaire britannique. Il y a de nombreuses années, cette ligne fut mise hors service pour des raisons économiques. Pourtant, les amoureux du chemin de fer remirent les vieilles locomotives à vapeur sur les rails et rouvrirent toutes les gares de la ligne en veillant à préserver le cachet de l'époque. Ces images montrent des volontaires au travail.

PAGE 107 Photographer: HOWARD SCHATZ Representative: BEVERLY ORNSTEIN Camera: HASSELBLAD Film: KODAK PLUS-X Art Director: HOWARD SCHATZ Country: USA ■ From a series of over 50 pregnant nudes, which were taken along with a complementing series of newborns. ● Das Bild gehört zu einer Reihe von 50 Aktporträts schwangerer Frauen. Dazu gehört eine Serie über Neugeborene. ▲ Image extraite d'une série de 50 nus de femmes enceintes. Une autre série était consacrée aux nouveaux-nés.

PAGE 108 Photographer: MANOLO GARCIA Representative: CATBIRD REPRESENTS/ CATHRYN BLUM Cameras: PENTAX 6x7, TOYO 4x5" Films: KODAK TRI-X, POLAROID 55PN Designer: MANOLO GARCIA Country: USA ■ "The Senses," images on the joy of anticipation and experience provided by the senses. For this series the film was purposely overexposed by two stops. The images were then printed in a way that would create hazy, abstract forms. ● «Die Sinne» – Bilder über den Genuss von sinnlicher Vorfreude und Erfahrung. Für diese Aufnahmen wurde der Film absichtlich um zwei Blenden überbelichtet. Bei den Abzügen kam es darauf an, unscharfe, abstrakte Formen zu erzielen. ▲ «Les sens». Images sur le plaisir des expériences et anticipations sensuelles. Le film a volontairement été surexposé lors des prises de vue et retravaillé au tirage pour obtenir des formes floues et abstraites.

PAGE 109 Photographer: PEGGY SIROTA Representative: ELYSE CONNOLLY Publisher: *BRITISH VOGUE* Art Directors: Robin Derrick, Robin Muir Country: Great Britain ■ British-born artist David Hockney in his California home. Although he sells his work for $500,000, he still considers himself "a working class hero." ● Der britische Künstler David Hockney in seinem kalifornischen Haus. Obgleich seine Bilder inzwischen eine halbe Million Dollar das Stück kosten, sieht er sich immer noch als «Working Class Hero». ▲ L'artiste britannique David Hockney dans sa résidence californienne. Bien que ses images se vendent aujourd'hui un demi million de dollars, il se considère toujours comme un «héros de la classe ouvrière».

PAGE 110 Photographer: AERNOUT OVERBEEKE Representatives: CHRISTA KLUBERT, GERMANY; FREDDY BRAZIL, GREAT BRITAIN; HILARY BRADFORD, ITALY Camera: ROLLEIFLEX Film: KODAK TRI-X Country: NETHERLANDS ■ Photo of a man sitting in the canteen of a steel factory in Poland, taken without his knowledge. ● Ein Mann in der Kantine einer polnischen Stahlfabrik. Er bemerkte den Photographen nicht. ▲ Homme attablé dans la cantine d'une aciérie polonaise, photographié à son insu.

PAGE 111 Photographer: AERNOUT OVERBEEKE Representatives: CHRISTA KLUBERT, GERMANY; FREDDY BRAZIL, GREAT BRITAIN; HILARY BRADFORD, ITALY Client: HEINEKEN Camera: SINAR Film: ILFORD XP2 Art Director: GERARD VAN DER HART Agency: PMS VW Y&R Country: NETHERLANDS ■ Image from a campaign for Amstel 1870 beer. The location, an old coal mine, and the clothes of the models allude to the "1870" of the brand name. ● Das Bild behört zu einer Kampagne für Amstel 1870 Bier. Der Ort, eine alte Kohlenmine, und die Kleidung der Modelle sind eine Anspielung auf das Jahr '1870' im Markennamen. ▲ Image d'une campagne publicitaire pour la bière Amstel 1870. Décor et vêtements évoquent l'année 1870.

PAGE 112 Photographer: DAVID POWERS Camera: MAMIYA RZ 67 Film: KODAK T-MAX 100 Art Director: GREG MILLER Agency: DDP Country: USA ■ Johnny Oliver, 85 years old, is a tall man, almost totally deaf, blind in both eyes, and walks with two canes. The photographer took his portrait because of the strength of character in his face. During the session Mr. Oliver told the photographer about walking the Burma Road in Malaysia during World War II. While he talked, he held his head high, as if he were seeing the whole experience over again. ● Johnny Oliver, 85 Jahre alt. Der grosse Mann geht an Krücken, ist fast völlig taub und auf beiden Augen blind. Der Photograph war von seinen charaktervollen Gesichtszügen fasziniert. Während der Aufnahmen erzählte der alte Mann von seiner Zeit als Soldat im zweiten Weltkrieg in Malaysia. Er sprach mit erhobenem Kopf und sah aus, als habe er das Geschehen wieder ganz nah vor Augen. ▲ Johnny Oliver, 85 ans. Aveugle, presque sourd, il ne se déplace qu'à l'aide de béquilles. Sa physionomie hors du commun fascina le photographe. Lors de la séance photo, le vieil homme relata ses souvenirs de la Seconde Guerre mondiale, la marche sur Malaka. Il parlait, la tête haute, et semblait revivre ces scènes du passé avec précision.

PAGE 113 Photographer: STEVE MARSEL Client: INK STONE PRESS, INC. Camera: HASSELBLAD 500 ELM Film: FUJI VELVIA 120 Exposure: F11/1/8 SEC. Art Director/Designer: LEIGHTON COLLIS Agency: THINK TANK Country: USA ■ A real card reader and a real used-car salesman were photographed for a promotional brochure for a small printer. The idea was to shoot people who have reputations for being dishonest, a reputation that is generally also attributed to printers. Of course, the printer in question claims to be different. ● Eine echte Wahrsagerin und ein echter Verkäufer gebrauchter Autos zierten die Werbebroschüre einer kleinen Druckerei. Die Idee war, Leute zu photographieren, die hinsichtlich ihrer Ehrlichkeit einen schlechten Ruf haben, wie ganz allgemein auch Druckereien. Diese bestimmte Druckerei besteht natürlich darauf, anders zu sein. ▲ Cette photo d'une cartomancienne et d'un vendeur de voitures d'occasion illustre la brochure publicitaire d'une petite imprimerie. L'idée était de mettre en scène des professions dont on conteste l'honnêteté. L'imprimerie entendait bien sûr se démarquer clairement par sa probité et la qualité de ses prestations.

PAGE 114 Photographer: JOSÉ PICAYO Representative: BARBARA VON SCHREIBER Publisher/Client: *ROLLING STONE/STRAIGHT ARROW PUBLISHERS* Art Director: FRED WOODWARD Photo Editor: JODI PECKMAN Designers: FRED WOODWARD, GAIL ANDERSON, GERALDINE HESSLER, LEE BEARSON Country: USA ■ Portrait of Natalie Merchant that appeared in a special issue of *Rolling Stone* entitled "Generation Next." The issue documented the current transformation of rock 'n' roll through portraits of artists who are, according to the magazine, the future of rock, "a generation that reflects on its experiences, addresses its problems, and expresses its hopes and fears." ● Porträt von Natalie Merchant, das in einer Spezialausgabe der Zeitschrift *Rolling Stone* mit dem Titel «Generation Next» erschien. Sie dokumentiert die Weiterentwicklung des Rock & Roll mit Porträts von Künstlern, die, nach Meinung der Redakteure die Zukunft des Rocks sind, eine «Generation, die ihre Erfahrungen verarbeitet, sich mit ihren Problemen befasst und ihren Hoffnungen und Ängsten Ausdruck verleiht». ▲ Portrait de Natalie Merchant, publié dans une édition spéciale du magazine *Rolling Stone* sous le titre «Generation Next». Consacré à l'évolution du Rock & Roll, ce numéro est illustré par les portraits des stars qui, selon l'avis du rédacteur, auront un impact décisif sur l'avenir du rock, et qui s'affirment comme une «génération en train d'assimiler les expériences acquises, qui s'attaque à ses problèmes et exprime ses peurs et ses espoirs.»

PAGE 115 Photographer: KENT BARKER Client: WARNER BROTHERS RECORDS Camera: HASSELBLAD ELX Film: KODAK T-MAX 100 Art Director: KIM CHAMPAGNE Country: USA ■ Portrait of Jerry Lee Lewis for an album cover. As he had just returned to the United States after living in Ireland for a couple of years, his belongings were still in the process of being shipped over when the shooting took place. He had few clothes and very little furniture in the States. A rental tuxedo was quickly delivered to the site, and a faux-French couch (one of his prized possessions) was taken outside to the edge of the lake behind his house—an idea that took his breath away for a moment. But then he decided that he loved it. ● Porträt von Jerry Lee Lewis für eine Plattenhülle. Da er zur Zeit der Aufnahme gerade nach einem längeren Aufenthalt in Irland in die USA zurückgekehrt war, war ein Grossteil seiner Besitztümer noch unterwegs. Es waren nur wenige Möbel und keine geeignete Kleidung vorhanden. So wurde schnell ein Smoking ausgeliehen, und ein Kanapee, der ganze Stolz seines Besitzers, wurde hinters Haus an das Ufer eines Sees transportiert – was Mr. Lewis für einen Moment die Sprache verschlug. Aber dann beschloss er, den Einfall prima zu finden. ▲ Portrait de Jerry Lee Lewis destiné à illustrer la pochette d'un disque. Comme il venait juste de rentrer aux USA après un long séjour en Irlande, la plupart de ses effets personnels n'étaient pas encore arrivés le jour de la séance photo. Pour remédier à la disparité du mobilier et à l'absence de vêtements adéquats, on décida de louer un smoking et de transporter l'un de ses canapés favoris derrière la maison, au bord d'un lac. D'abord légèrement déconcerté, M. Lewis fut finalement séduit par l'idée.

PAGE 116 Photographer: MARC NORBERG Camera: HASSELBLAD Film: KODAK PLUS-X 120 Art Director: MARC NORBERG Country: USA ■ Image from a series on babies, photographed within seven days after their birth. ● Das Bild gehört zu einer Photoserie über Neugeborene in den ersten sieben Tagen nach ihrer Geburt. ▲ Image extraite d'une série sur des nouveaux-nés photographiés quelques jours après leur naissance.

PAGE 117 Photographer: LISA SPINDLER Representative: MICHAEL ASH Camera: NIKON F3 Film: AGFACHROME 1000 Country: USA ■ A painterly look in a beauty shot taken for the photographer's portfolio. ● Bei dieser freien Beauty-Aufnahme ging es um der Photographin um den gemäldeähnlichen Effekt. ▲ Pour cette photo de mode, l'artiste s'attacha à capturer la beauté picturale de son sujet.

PAGE 118 Photographer: ABHIJIT VARDE Client: CREATIVITY EXPLORED OF SAN FRANCISCO Camera: SINAR F1 Film: KODAK TRI-X Exposure: F16/15 Art Director: ABHIJIT VARDE Country: USA ■ The photographer volunteered as a photography teacher at an institute for the arts supporting the mentally disabled. These portraits of his students were shown in a fund-raising exhibition together with their work. ● Der Photograph unterrichtete Photographie an einem Kunstinstitut zur Unterstützung geistig Behinderter. Diese Porträts seiner Schüler wurden zusammen mit ihren eigenen Arbeiten in einer Benefiz-Ausstellung gezeigt. ▲ Le photographe enseigna bénévolement la photographie dans un institut d'art soutenant des handicapés. Les travaux et les portraits de ses élèves furent exposés dans le cadre d'une œuvre de bienfaisance.

PAGE 119 (top) Photographer: HARRY DE ZITTER Camera: LINHOF TECHNORAMA 6x12 Film: FUJI VELVIA 120 Exposures: F11/1/15 SEC., F16/1/15 SEC. Art Director: HARRY DE ZITTER Country: USA ■ "Pete, the birdhouse man," from Maine. The photographer met him by chance while driving around. Since the shot was taken, they have spoken every few months. ● «Pete, der Vogelhausmann» aus Maine. Seit der Photograph ihn zufällig bei einer Reise entdeckte, sprechen sie hin und wieder miteinander. ▲ «Pete, l'oiselier» du Maine. Depuis leur rencontre fortuite lors d'un voyage, le photographe entretient des contacts réguliers avec lui.

PAGE 119 (bottom) Photographer: HARRY DE ZITTER Camera: LINHOF TECHNORAMA 6x12 Film: FUJI VELVIA 120 Exposures: F11/1/15 SEC., F16/1/15 SEC. Art Director: HARRY DE ZITTER Country: USA ■ This vehicle used to be an ambulance but the owner decided to make a pick-up truck out of it. The photograph was made in Texas one foggy morning, which provided a beautiful quality of light. ● Das Fahrzeug war ursprünglich ein Ambulanzwagen, bevor sein Besitzer es in einen Lastwagen umbaute. Die Aufnahme entstand an einem nebligen Morgen in Texas, der dem Bild die besondere Lichtqualität gab. ▲ Ambulance transformée en camion par les soins de son propriétaire. L'image a été prise au Texas, lors d'un matin brumeux qui permit d'obtenir cette lumière exceptionnelle.

PAGES 120, 121 Photographer: HERB RITTS Representative: VISAGES Publisher/Client: *ROLLING STONE/STRAIGHT ARROW PUBLISHERS* Art Director: FRED WOODWARD Photo

Editor: LAURIE KRATOCHVIL Country: USA ■ Supermodel, MTV hostess, Revlon girl Cindy Crawford, photographed by Herb Ritts for *Rolling Stone*. ● Das amerikanische Supermodell, MTV-Hostess und Revlon-Frau Cindy Crawford, aufgenommen von Herb Ritts für *Rolling Stone*. ▲ Mannequin star, présentatrice sur MTV et ambassadrice de la marque Revlon, Cindy Crawford, photographiée par Herb Ritts pour le magazine *Rolling Stone*.

PAGE 122 Photographer: MARC NORBERG Client: NATIONAL EASTER SEAL SOCIETY Camera: HASSELBLAD Film: KODAK PLUS-X Art Director/Designer: PETE GRIFFITH Agency: CME KHBB ADVERTISING Country: USA ■ Portrait of Colleen Flanagan for a National Easter Seal Society ad campaign on their 75th anniversary. The organization provides rehabilitation and support services to people with disabilities. ● Porträt eines kleinen Mädchens für eine Werbekampagne zum 75jährigen Bestehen einer Gesellschaft, die Rehabilitationseinrichtungen und Dienstleistungen für Behinderte anbietet. ▲ Portrait d'une fillette pour une campagne publicitaire lancée à l'occasion du 75ème anniversaire d'une société spécialisée dans des équipements de rééducation et des prestations pour handicapés.

PAGE 123 Photographer: RON BAXTER SMITH Publisher/Client: *GQ*/THE CONDE NAST PUBLICATIONS INC. Camera: SINAR 4x5 Film: POLAROID TYPE 55 Art Directors: ROBERT PRIEST, LAURA HARRIGAN Designer: LAURA HARRIGAN Country: USA ■ "The Oyes of Sex" or "Love Hurts." This photograph was taken for an article in *Gentleman's Quarterly* on physical injuries sustained during sexual pursuits. ● «Liebe tut weh.» Die Verletzungen, die man sich beim Sex zuziehen kann, waren Thema eines Artikels in der Zeitschrift *Gentleman's Quarterly*. ▲ «Lorsque l'amour fait mal.» Les blessures pouvant être occasionnées par certaines pratiques sexuelles firent l'objet d'un article publié dans le magazine *Gentleman's Quaterly*.

PAGE 124 Photographer: ROSANNE OLSON Camera: 4x5" Film: POLAROID TYPE 55 Art Director: ROSANNE OLSON Country: USA ■ Image from a series of angel portraits that the photographer took of a friend with AIDS. ● Das Bild gehört zu einer Serie von Engelporträts, die die Photographin von einem an AIDS erkrankten Freund machte. ▲ Image extraite d'une série de portraits d'anges. Le sujet, malade du sida, est un ami de la photographe.

PAGE 125 Photographer: MARK HANAUER Representative: ONYX Publisher: *ENTERTAINMENT WEEKLY* Camera: MAMIYA 645 Film: FUJI RHP Picture Editors: DORIS BRAUTIGAN, BETH TAUBNER Country: USA ■ Portrait of film director Oliver Stone. ● Porträt des Filmregisseurs Oliver Stone. ▲ Portrait du réalisateur Oliver Stone.

PAGE 126 Photographer: TERRY HUSEBYE Representative: ARLENE JOHNSON Client: LUXOR HOTEL + CASINO Camera: NIKON F4 Film: FUJI RDP Exposure: F5.6 1/2/1/250 Art Director: JOAN LYONS Agency: GSD&M Country: USA ■ The various facilities of the Luxor Hotel and Casino in Las Vegas were documented in ads, billboards, and brochures. Instead of the usual chaise lounge views of pools, the photographer did above/below water pictures. ● Die verschiedenen Einrichtungen des Luxor Hotels und Casinos in Las Vegas waren Gegenstand von Anzeigen, Billboardwerbung und Broschüren. Anstelle der üblichen Liegestuhlaufnahmen zeigte der Photograph den Pool in verschiedenen Über- und Unterwasseraufnahmen. ▲ Les luxueux équipements de l'hôtel Luxor et du casino de Las Vegas firent l'objet de nombreuses publicités, affiches et brochures. En lieu et place des traditionnelles chaises longues, le photographe prit divers clichés sous-marins et panoramiques de la piscine.

PAGE 127 Photographer: BOB FRAME Representative: PROOF Publisher: *PREMIERE* MAGAZINE Camera: PENTAX 6x7 Film: KODAK TRI-X Art Director: JOHN KORPICS Picture Editor: CHARLIE HOLLAND Country: USA ■ An unpublished portrait of actor Johnny Depp. He was a photographer's dream shoot—no idea was too weird that he wouldn't work through. ● Ein unveröffentlichtes Porträt des Schauspielers Johnny Depp. Er erwies sich als Traumpartner eines Photographen: keine Idee war zu ausgefallen, als dass er nicht mitgemacht hätte. ▲ Portrait non publié de l'acteur Johnny Depp. Modèle de rêve de tout photographe, aucune suggestion ne lui semble trop saugrenue.

PAGE 128 Photographer: STEPHANIE PFRIENDER Representative: JUDY CASEY Publisher: *ENTERTAINMENT WEEKLY* Camera: NIKON F3 Film: KODAK EKTACHROME 400 Exposure: F5.6/1/15 sec. Art Director: DORIS BRAUTIGAN Photography Director: MARY DUNN Associate Picture Editor: RAMIRO FERNANDEZ Country: USA ■ Portrait of David Thewlis for *Entertainment Weekly*. He is the type that would be perfect as a Hitchcock character—indeed the bathroom at the old hotel in New York felt as if a mystery were lurking behind

the door. The cold colors add to the desolate mood. ● Porträt des britischen Filmschauspielers David Thewlis, der ausgezeichnet in einen Hitchcock-Film passen würde. Tatsächlich hatte das Badezimmer in dem alten New Yorker Hotel etwas Unheimliches, als wenn etwas hinter der Tür lauern würde. Die kalten Farben förderten diesen Eindruck noch. ▲ Portrait de l'acteur britannique David Thewlis, semblant sortir tout droit d'un film d'Hitchcock. Cette impression est encore renforcée par la salle de bains du vieil hôtel new-yorkais et la froideur des lieux qui accentuent l'atmosphère sordide et inquiétante.

PAGE 129 Photographer: DENNIS MANARCHY Camera: HASSELBLAD Film: ILFORD Exposure: F2.8 1/2/2 sec. Art Director: DAVID JENKINS Designer: BILL SOSIN Country: USA ■ Photograph from a series of portraits of the Chicago homeless created for an exhibition and a book, the revenues of which went to the homeless. The portraits were accompanied by quotes from the homeless replying to the question "What do you think of before going to sleep?" ● Diese Aufnahme gehört zu einer Porträtreihe der Obdachlosen von Chicago. Die Porträts wurden in einer Ausstellung und einem Buch gezeigt, wobei die Einnahmen den Obdachlosen zugute kamen. Die Antworten der Obdachlosen auf die Frage, woran sie vor dem Einschlafen dächten, begleiteten die Porträts. ▲ Image extraite d'une série de portraits sur les sans-abri de Chicago, réalisée pour une exposition et un livre dans le cadre d'une œuvre de bienfaisance au bénéfice des S.D.F. La réponse des sans-abri à la question «A quoi pensez-vous avant de vous endormir?» servit de légende aux portraits.

PAGE 130 Photographer: ACHIM DETERDING Camera: HASSELBLAD 500C Film: KODAK T-MAX 100 Exposure: DAYLIGHT 1/30 sec. Country: GERMANY ■ "Grand, 26.8.1991," portrait of the photographer's grandmother on the day before her 86th birthday. ● «Grand, 26.8.1991», Porträt der Grossmutter des Photographen am Tag vor ihrem 86. Geburtstag. ▲ «Grand, 26.8.1991». Portrait de la grand-mère du photographe le jour de son 86e anniversaire.

PAGE 131 Photographer: LISA SPINDLER Representative: MICHAEL ASH Client: RHODE ISLAND COUNCIL ON ALCOHOLISM Camera: NIKON F3 Art Director: ROB RICH Agency: LEONARD, MONAHAN, LUBARS, KELLY Country: USA ■ Unpublished photograph from a series on pregnancy done for a council on alcoholism. This shot was done with natural light. ● Unveröffentlichte Aufnahme aus einer Serie über Schwangerschaft im Auftrag einer Beratungsstelle für Alkoholiker. Die Photographin arbeitete mit Tageslicht. ▲ Photo non publiée extraite d'une série sur la grossesse, réalisée pour un centre de consultation pour alcooliques. La photo a été prise à la lumière du jour.

PAGE 132 Photographer: DIETER BLUM Publisher/Client: STERN/GRUNER + JAHR Camera: LEICA R7 Film: AGFACHROME 200 Art Director: WOLFGANG BEHNKEN Designer: SANDRA KAISER Country: GERMANY ■ Artist and model, an old subject interpreted in an unusual way. Photographer Dieter Blum asked 15 painters to integrate the model into a work of art. Shown is artist Ben Willikens from Stuttgart and his model in his studio with his paintings, which are usually devoid of people. ● Künstler und Modell, das uralte Thema auf ganz neue Art interpretiert. Der Photograph Dieter Blum bat 15 Künstler, das Modell selbst zum Kunstwerk zu machen. Hier der Stuttgarter Maler Ben Willikens mit seinem Modell und seinen sonst menschenleeren, nüchternen Raumbildern. ▲ L'artiste et son modèle, un sujet classique interprété sous un jour nouveau. Le photographe Dieter Blum demanda à 15 artistes de placer leur sujet au centre de leur œuvre afin d'en faire l'essence même de l'œuvre. Sur la présente photo, l'artiste-peintre Ben Willikens en compagnie de son modèle dans son atelier de Stuttgart avec ses toiles, dont l'être humain est d'habitude banni.

PAGE 133 Photographer: PETER KELIH Camera: MAMIYA RZ 67 Film: KODAK TMX 100 Exposure: F5.6/1/8 sec. Country: AUSTRIA ■ The tenderness of young love expressed through distorted movement. The photographer worked with long exposure: 1/8 sec. with camera in hand. To light the scene, he directed the headlight straight onto cardboard. ● Die Zärtlichkeit junger Liebe, ausgedrückt mit Hilfe von Bewegungsunschärfe. Für seine Aufnahme arbeitete der Photograph mit langer Belichtungszeit: 1/8 sec. aus der Hand. Beleuchtet wurde die Szene durch direkt auf einen Karton gerichtetes Licht. ▲ Tendresse des premières amours, exprimée par le flou. Pour obtenir ce résultat, le photographe travailla sans pied avec un temps de pose de 1/8 seconde. Pour éclairer la scène, il braqua une lampe sur un carton.

PAGE 134 (top) Photographer: MARK SELIGER Representative: PROOF Client: VIRGIN RECORDS Camera: 4x5" Art Director: LEN PELTIER Country: USA ■ Keith Richards and Mick Jagger photographed for the Rolling Stones's Vodoo Lounge Tour. ● Keith Richards und Mick Jagger, für eine Tournee der Rolling Stones photographiert. ▲ Keith Richards et Mick Jagger, photographiés pour une tournée des Rolling Stones.

PAGE 134 (bottom), **PAGE 135** (bottom) Photographer: MARK SELIGER Representative: PROOF Publisher: *US MAGAZINE* Cameras: MAMIYA 6X7 (3, 4), PENTAX 6X7 (7), TOYA 4X5" (8) FILMS: KODAK TRI-X (3, 4, 7), FUJI RDP (7, 8) Photo Editors: RACHEL KNEPFER (3, 4), JENNIFER CRANDALL (7, 8) Art Director: RICHARD BAKER (3, 4, 7) Country: USA ■ Portraits of actress Drew Barrymore, Oscar-award winner Tom Hanks, and musician Jackson Browne for *US Magazine*. ● Porträts der Schauspielerin Drew Barrymore, des Oscar-Preisträgers Tom Hanks und des Pop-Stars Jackson Browne für *US Magazine*. ▲ Portraits de l'actrice Drew Barrymore, de l'acteur Tom Hanks et de la vedette pop Jackson Browne réalisés pour *US Magazine*.

PAGE 135 (top) Photographer: MARK SELIGER Representative: PROOF Publisher/Client: *ROLLING STONE*/STRAIGHT ARROW PUBLISHERS Cameras: MAMIYA 6X7 (5), PENTAX 6X7 (6) Films: FUJI RDP (5), KODAK TRI-X (6) Art Director: FRED WOODWARD Photo Editors: JODI PECKMAN (5), PATTI O'BRIEN (6) Country: USA ■ John Mellencamp and Cassandra Williams, photographed for *Rolling Stone* magazine. ● John Mellencamp und Cassandra Williams, für *Rolling Stone* porträtiert. ▲ Portraits de John Mellencamp et Cassandra Williams réalisés pour le magazine *Rolling Stone*.

PAGE 136 Photographer: HOWARD SCHATZ Representative: BEVERLY ORNSTEIN Client: GRAPHIS PRESS CORP. Camera: NIKONOS R5 Film: KODAK UNDERWATER Art Director/Designer: HOWARD SCHATZ Book Editor: B. MARTIN PEDERSEN Country: USA ■ Image from the series "Water Dance." Shown is Katita Waldo, a principal dancer of the San Francisco Ballet. ● Aufnahme aus einer Reihe mit dem Titel «Water Dance». Hier eine der ersten Tänzerinnen des San Francisco Ballet, Katita Waldo. ▲ Image extraite d'une série intitulée «Water Dance». Le sujet, Katita Waldo, fut l'une des premières danseuses du Ballet de San Francisco.

PAGE 137 Photographer: KENJI TOMA Representative: MICHAEL ASH Client/Agency: CHIC SIMPLE Camera: HORSEMAN 4X5" Film: KODAK VHC Art Director: JEFF STONE Designer: ROBERT VALENTINE Country: USA ■ Image from the *Body Book*. ● Aufnahme aus einem Buch mit dem Titel *Body Book*. ▲ Image extraite du livre *Body Book*.

PAGE 138 Photographer: NEIL BECKERMAN Camera: MAMIYA RZ 67 Film: POLAROID 665 Exposure: F8/400 Art Director: NEIL BECKERMAN Country: USA ■ "Lindsay," an image from a series of portraits of New Yorkers. Lindsay is very involved in the reggae club scene. ● «Lindsay», Porträt aus einer Serie über New Yorker. Lindsay ist eine wichtige Figur in der Reggae-Szene. ▲ «Lindsay». Image d'une série de portraits sur des personnages new-yorkais. Lindsay est une personnalité incontournable de la scène reggae.

PAGE 139 Photographer: DAN BORRIS Representative: EDGE Publisher/Client: *ROLLING STONE*/STRAIGHT ARROW PUBLISHERS Art Director: FRED WOODWARD Photo Editor: JODI PECKMAN Designers: FRED WOODWARD, GAIL ANDERSON, GERALDINE HESSLER, LEE BEARSON Country: USA ■ "Babes in Toyland"—from top to bottom: Maureen Herman, Kat Bjelland, and Lori Barbero. Portraits from "Generation Next," a special issue of *Rolling Stone* featuring the most promising stars of the rock 'n' roll scene. ● «Babes in Toyland» – von oben nach unten: Maureen Herman, Kat Bjelland und Lori Barbero. Die Porträts stammen aus einer Spezialnummer der Zeitschrift *Rolling Stone*, die den neuen Stars des Rock and Roll gewidmet ist. ▲ «Babes in Toyland» – de haut en bas: Maureen Herman, Kat Bjelland et Lori Barbero. Photos extraites d'un numéro spécial du magazine *Rolling Stone* consacré aux nouvelles stars du rock & roll.

PAGE 140 Photographer: ENRIQUE BADULESCU Representatives: GIOVANNI TESTINO, USA, MICHELE FILOMENO, EUROPE Camera: KONICA PRESS Country: USA ■ Personal collage made up of outtakes from different shoots. ● Die Aufnahme dieser persönlichen Collage des Photographen sind Bilder, die am Rande verschiedener Aufträge entstanden sind. ▲ Les images de ce collage ont été prises dans le cadre de prises de vue réalisées par le photographe.

PAGE 141 Photographer: FABRIZIO FERRI Representative: ART + COMMERCE Client: L'ORÉAL Country: Europe ■ Image used in an ad for L'Oréal cosmetics. ● Diese Aufnahme wurde in einer Anzeige für L'Oréal verwendet. ▲ Cette image fut utilisée pour une publicité L'Oréal.

PAGE 142 Photographer: RJ MUNA Country: USA ■ Example from a personal series on faces. ● Beispiel aus einer freien Reihe über Gesichter. ▲ Exemple d'une série libre sur des visages.

PAGE 143 Photographer: LISA SPINDLER Representative: MICHAEL ASH Client: BOSWELL HATS Camera: NIKON F3 Country: USA ■ Promotional shot for a hatmaker. A plastic hat was photographed and later manipulated. ● Eine Werbeaufnahme für einen Hutmacher. Es handelte sich um einen Plastikhut, der photographiert und später manipuliert wurde. ▲ Photo publicitaire réalisée pour un chapelier. Le chapeau, en plastique, a été retravaillé ultérieurement sur ordinateur.

PAGE 144 Photographer: GEORGE PETRAKES Representative: MARY JANE Cameras: NIKON F3 (BABY), MAMIYA 645 (PRODUCT) Films: KODAK RECORDING FILM (BABY), FUJI RDP 100 (PRODUCT) Exposures: F16/60 (BABY), F11/25 (PRODUCT) Art Director/Designer: GEORGE PETRAKES Country: USA ■ Double images are typical of the photographer. The baby was shot with black-and-white film, which was then toned to obtain layers of blue and copper. The pacifiers were shot in color, then cross-processed C-41 normal and printed so that the two images would work as a whole. ● Doppelbilder wie dieses sind das Markenzeichen des Photographen. Das Baby wurde mit einem Schwarzweissfilm aufgenommen und dann getönt, um Schichten von Blau und Kupfer zu erhalten. Die Schnuller wurden in Farbe photographiert und dann nach der Umkehrentwicklung mit C-41 so abgezogen, dass die beiden Bilder zusammen die gewünschte Wirkung ergaben. ▲ Les images doubles sont récurrentes dans l'œuvre du photographe. Le bébé a été photographié avec un film noir et blanc ultérieurement viré pour obtenir des couches de bleu et de cuivre. Les tétines ont été prises avec un film couleur puis, après le développement inversé C-41, tirées de manière à ce que les deux images forment un tout.

PAGE 145 Photographer: MARK SELIGER Representative: PROOF Publisher/Client: *ROLLING STONE*/STRAIGHT ARROW PUBLISHERS Camera: MAMIYA 6X7 Film: KODAK TRI-X Art Director: FRED WOODWARD Photo Editor: LAURIE KRATOCHVIL Country: USA ■ Portrait of Curtis Mayfield for *Rolling Stone* magazine. ● Porträt von Curtis Mayfield für die Zeitschrift *Rolling Stone*. ▲ Portrait de Curtis Mayfield pour le magazine *Rolling Stone*.

PAGE 146 Photographer: RICHARD J. BURBRIDGE Representative: TOM BOOTH Publisher/Client: *VOGUE*/THE CONDÉ NAST PUBLICATIONS INC. Art Director: RAUL MARTINEZ Fashion Editor: CANDY PRATTS PRICE Country: USA ■ Platinum sunglasses, available at Cartier boutiques for about $495 The shot was taken for a fashion feature in American *Vogue*. ● Platin-Sonnenbrillen, in Cartier Boutiquen für ca. $495 erhältlich. Die Aufnahme gehört zu einem Modebeitrag in der amerikanischen *Vogue*. ▲ Lunettes de soleil en platine, disponibles dans les boutiques Cartier moyennant 495 dollars. Cette photo a été publiée dans l'édition américaine de *Vogue*.

PAGES 148, 149 Photographer: CONNY J. WINTER Client: PORSCHE AG Camera: NIKON F4 Film: FUJI VELVIA Art Director/Designer: CONNY J. WINTER Country: GERMANY ■ At left: the glamorous introduction of the first Porsche Carrera cabriolet, from the assembly line directly to this scene, a festive act that included the ballet of Stuttgart and a fashion show. At right: A photograph from a Porsche calendar entitled "Enjoying Performance" in which owners of a Porsches are shown in action on location. ● Links: ein glanzvoller Auftritt des ersten Porsche Carrera Cabriolets – vom Fliessband direkt auf die Bühne – im Rahmen eines Festprogramms mit dem Stuttgarter Ballett und einer Modenschau. Rechts: eine Aufnahme aus dem Porschekalender «Enjoying Performance», für den Porschefahrer bei ihrem Sport an Originalschauplätzen live photographiert wurden. ▲ A gauche: l'entrée en scène remarquée du premier cabriolet Porsche Carrera – sorti tout droit des ateliers de production – lors d'une manifestation spéciale avec un défilé de mode et un spectacle du ballet de Stuttgart. A droite: l'une des photos du calendrier Porsche «Enjoying Performance» représentant des conducteurs de Porsche dans le feu de l'action.

PAGE 150 Photographer: NATALIE BOEHM Camera: NIKON 8008 Film: POLAROID POLAGRAPH Art Director/Designer: NATALIE BOEHM Country: USA ■ The photographer took advantage of the contrast of the Polaroid Polagraph film to accentuate the graphic sense of the car and to create a sense of antiquity. ● Die Photographin nutzte die Kontraststärke des Polaroid Polagraph-Films, um die graphische Wirkung zu verstärken und ein Gefühl von Gediegenheit zu erzeugen. ▲ Pour accentuer l'effet graphique de l'habitacle tout en rendant une atmosphère chaleureuse, l'artiste s'est servi d'un film Polaroid Polagraph à forts contrastes.

PAGE 151 Photographer: RON FEHLING Client: TOSHIBA Camera: POLAROID 600 Film: POLAROID 665 Art Director: DUNCAN BRUCE Agency: CHIAT DAY Country: CANADA ■ Part of a campaign illustrating the durability of Toshiba computers. The car was pushed slightly forward to give the viewer a feeling of motion. ● Diese Aufnahme gehört zu einer Werbekampagne, in der die Robustheit von Toshiba-Computern demonstriert werden soll. Das Auto wurde leicht angeschoben, um dem Betrachter das Gefühl von Bewegung zu geben. ▲ Cette photo fut utilisée pour une campagne publicitaire destinée à vanter la robustesse des ordinateurs Toshiba. En poussant légèrement la voiture lors de la prise de vue, on a obtenu une impression de mouvement.

PAGE 152 Photographer: RIAN HORN Camera: CANON A1 Film: AGFA XRG 100 Exposure: F16 Country: SOUTH AFRICA ■ The photograph was taken in South Africa's winter months when the color of the grass turns to pale yellow. The dark yellow color was achieved through the help of a strong wind and the low color temperature of tungsten light, with a time exposure of 20 minutes on the grass alone. The red interior was also artificially lit with a flash, balanced out with tungsten light in the background. The red interior as well as the grass were enhanced by using a red and yellow filter respectively on the first couple of flashes used. ● Die Aufnahme wurde während der Wintermonate in Südafrika gemacht, wenn das Gras eine hellgelbe Färbung annimmt. Unterstützt durch einen starken Wind und die tiefe Farbtemperatur des Tungstenlichtes, wurde das satte Gelb des Grases durch zwanzigminütige Belichtung erzielt. Das rote Interieur des Autos wurde ebenfalls künstlich mit Blitz belichtet, der durch Tungstenlicht im Hintergrund ausbalanciert wurde. Das Rot und das Gelb wurden durch Rot- bzw. Gelbfilter auf den ersten paar Blitzen verstärkt. ▲ Cette photo a été prise en Afrique du Sud, en hiver, lorsque l'herbe se pare d'une teinte jaune pâle. Aidé par un fort vent et le tungstène – dont la couleur de la lumière est basse – le photographe a obtenu ce jaune intense après un temps de pose de 20 minutes. L'intérieur rouge de la voiture a également été éclairé au flash, équilibré à l'arrière-plan par un balayage effectué avec une lampe au tungstène. L'intensité des couleurs a été renforcée par l'utilisation de filtres jaune et rouge lors des premiers flashes.

PAGE 153 Photographer: DÖRFEL & KUHN FOTODESIGN Representative: MARTIN ZEISER Client: DELTA SPORTS GMBH Camera: SINAR P Film: KODAK EKTA 100 ROLLFILM 120 Exposure: F16 2/3/1/60 Designer: DÖRFEL & KUHN FOTODESIGN Country: GERMANY ■ Photo used in an advertising campaign for bicycles. An interesting visual approach (like focusing on details, light impressions, and unusual viewpoints) in presenting the bicycles was requested to attract the attention and arouse the curiosity of new consumer groups. ● Die Aufnahme gehört zu einer Anzeigenkampagne für Fahrräder. Durch die Gestaltung (spezielle Blickwinkel, Ausschnitte und Lichtsituation) sollte die Aufmerksamkeit und Neugier von neuen Kundenzielgruppen geweckt werden. ▲ Cette photo fut utilisée pour la campagne publicitaire d'une marque de bicyclettes. Il s'agissait d'éveiller l'intérêt de nouveaux groupes de consommateurs par des effets spéciaux (gros plans, angles de vue originaux, utilisation de la lumière).

PAGE 154 Photographer: HARRY DE ZITTER Client: JEVER BRAUEREI Camera: PENTAX 6x7 Film: FUJI VELVIA 120 Exposure: F4/125 Art Director: DENEKE V. WELDZIEN Agency: JUNG V. MATT Country: GERMANY ■ Borkum Island in the North Sea. The special feel of this part of Germany, called "Ostfriesland," was captured for the client, a beer brewery in this region. ● Die Insel Borkum. Die Aufnahme gehört zu einer Reihe für die Jever Brauerei, in der es um die besondere Stimmung der ostfriesischen Landschaft geht. ▲ L'île de Borkum, dans la mer du Nord. Extraite d'une série réalisée pour les bières Jever, cette photo illustre un paysage typique de la Frise orientale.

PAGES 156, 157 Photographer: INTAE KIM Client: AVALANCHE PUBLISHING Cameras: MAMIYA RB 67, ASAHIPENTAX 67 Film: KODAK T-MAX Exposure: F32/60 Art Director: INTAE KIM Country; USA ■ Photograph showing the rhythm of sand dunes in the first light of the early morning. These breathtaking photographs were taken in the California desert. ● Der Rhythmus von Sanddünen im ersten Licht des frühen Morgens. Diese atemberaubenden Bilder entstanden in der Wüste Kaliforniens. ▲ Dunes de sable mouvantes, au lever du jour. Ces images d'une beauté saisissante ont été prises dans le désert californien.

PAGE 158 Photographer: PETER ECKERT Camera: RAPID OMEGA Film: AGFAPAN 100 Country: USA ■ Chicago has 14 miles of lakefront within its city limits. Tens of thousands of people enjoy themselves here by day; at night, however, they are gone, and what is left is a stark essence with subdued energy." ● Ein ca. 20 km langer Uferstreifen des Michigansees gehört zum Stadtgebiet von Chicago. Am Tage vergnügen sich hier Zehntausende Menschen, aber nachts ist das Ufer menschenleer, und es gehört in seiner Reinheit wieder der Natur. ▲ La ville de Chicago s'étend sur plus de 20 km le long des rives du lac Michigan. Lieu de divertissement pour des milliers de personnes la journée, ses rivages redeviennent déserts la nuit tombée, dégageant une force inhabituelle.

PAGE 159 Photographer: MIKE SALISBURY Client: TAVARUA ISLAND SURF CO. Camera: OLYMPUS LS-3 Film: FUJI VELVIA 50 Exposure: F4.5/1/8 SEC. Art Director: MIKE SALISBURY Designer/Agency: MIKE SALISBURY COMMUNICATIONS INC. Country: USA ■ A small island of Fiji. The photographer waited several days until the sky clouded over, and for a brief moment, the permanent blue of sky and water disappeared. The image was to be used to promote the island. ● Eine kleine Insel, die zur Fidschi-Gruppe im Südpazifik gehört. Der Photograph wartete Tage, bis sich der Himmel für kurze Zeit bewölkte und das Blau in Blau von Himmel und Wasser für einen Moment verschwinden liess. Es ging um Werbung für diese Insel, um das Wesen des Südpazifiks. ▲ Petite île de l'archipel des Fidji, dans l'océan Pacifique du Sud-Ouest. Le photographe dut patienter plusieurs jours avant que des nuages n'obscurcissent un bref instant le bleu immuable du ciel et de la mer. Cette image était destinée à promouvoir l'île sur le plan touristique.

PAGE 160 Photographer: KENT BARKER Publisher: *MEN'S JOURNAL* MAGAZINE Camera: FUJI GX-680 Film: KODAK T-MAX 100 Art Director: MARK DANZIG Photo Editor: DEBORAH NEEDLEMAN Country: USA ■ Photo from a story in *Men's Journal* tracing the historic Old West haunts of Billy the Kid. The specific theme was a road trip from Silver City to Lincoln, New Mexico. The assignment requested simple, rustic images that would suggest the wide open spaces of the West. The vision of the train tracks vanishing into the empty landscape excited the photographer. He purposely underexposed and then overdeveloped the negative, thus increasing the contrast of the scene, deepening the blacks, and really popping out the tracks. ● Diese Aufnahme gehört zu einer Geschichte in *Men's Journal* auf den Spuren des legendären Wild-West-Helden Billy the Kid. Es ging darum, in einfachen Aufnahmen die Weite und Offenheit der Landschaft Neumexikos einzufangen. Der Anblick der sich in der Ferne verlierenden Bahnschienen begeisterte den Photographen. Durch absichtliche Unterbelichtung und anschliessende gesteigerte Entwicklung des Negativs verstärkte er die Kontraste: die Schwarztöne wurden vertieft, so dass die Schienen zum herausragenden Element wurden. ▲ Cette photo illustre une histoire publiée dans le magazine *Men's Journal* qui invitait le lecteur à partir sur les traces de Billy the Kid, légendaire héros du Far West. Il s'agissait de refléter l'immensité des paysages du Nouveau Mexique par des images simples. La vue de ces rails qui se perdent dans le lointain enchanta le photographe. Il renforça les contrastes en sous-exposant volontairement son sujet puis en surdéveloppant le négatif: les noirs, plus denses, font ressortir les rails qui deviennent l'élément central de l'image.

PAGE 161 Photographer: FABRIZIO FERRI Representative: ART + COMMERCE Client/Publisher: BLENHEIM GROUP USA, INC./NEW YORK PREMIER COLLECTIONS Creative Director: MADDALENA GRACIS Designer: GIANNI GIULIANELLI Agency: KAPPA GRAPHIC DESIGN STUDIO Country: USA ■ Photograph from a catalog for the New York Premier Collections, an international fashion trade show. The image of a beach is meant to represent swimwear. ● Aufnahme aus einem Katalog für die New York Premier Collections, eine internationale Modemesse. Das Bild vom Strand steht für Bademode. ▲ Image extraite d'un catalogue pour un salon international de mode, le New York Premier Collections. Cette photo illustrait la mode plage de la saison.

PAGE 162 Photographer: AERNOUT OVERBEEKE Representatives: CHRISTA KLUBERT, GERMANY; FREDDY BRAZIL, GREAT BRITAIN, HILARY BRADFORD, ITALY Publisher/Client: *AVENUE*/DE GEÏLLUSTREERDE PERS BV Camera: HASSELBLAD SWC Film: KODAK TRI-X Art Director: HANS VAN BLOMMESTEIN Country: NETHERLANDS ■ "Amelia Island, Florida." Image from a series assigned by *Avenue* magazine on the east coast of the United States, from Miami to New York. ● «Amelia Island, Florida.» Dieses Bild gehört zu einer Serie für die Zeitschrift *Avenue* über die Ostküste der USA, von Miami bis hinauf nach New York. ▲ «Amelia Island, Floride.» Publiée dans le magazine *Avenue*, cette photo fait partie d'une série destinée à illustrer un article sur la côte Est des Etats-Unis, de Miami à New York.

PAGE 163 Photographer: CHRISTOPHER THOMAS Representative: DAGMAR STAUDENMAIER Client: SCHLOSSBERG BETTWÄSCHE Camera: NIKON F4 Film: POLAGRAPH Art Director: FELIX ZIMMERMANN Agency: FARNER PUBLICIS Country: GERMANY ■ Photograph of a palm tree used in an advertising campaign for bed linen. Images of plants are associated with the prints on the fabrics. ● Diese Aufnahme einer Palme gehört zu einer Werbekampagne für Bettwäsche, in der Pflanzenaufnahmen assoziativ zum Dessin der Bettwäsche eingesetzt wurden. ▲ Photo tirée d'une campagne publicitaire réalisée pour des draps et des taies d'oreiller. L'objectif était de créer un lien entre le palmier et le motif des tissus.

PAGE 164 Photographer: SALLY GALL Publisher/Client: *TRAVEL HOLIDAY MAGAZINE/READER'S DIGEST PUBLICATIONS* Camera: HASSELBLAD Film: KODAK TRI-X PAN Director of Photography: BILL BLACK Art Director: LOU DILORENZO Photo Editor: STEPHANIE ANNE SYROP Photo Coordinator: SANDY PEREZ Country: USA ■ The coastline of Block Island, Rhode Island. Image from a series for *Travel Holiday Magazine* entitled "American Moments." The photo was taken late in the day in May; although it was almost summer, the beach still lay in a grey, wintery mood of solitude and beauty. ● Die Küste von Block Island, Rhode Island, New York. Das Bild gehört zu einer Serie mit dem Titel «American Moments» für *Travel Holiday Magazine*. Es entstand an einem Spätnachmittag im Mai, aber am Strand herrschte noch der Winter in seiner grauen Einsamkeit und Schönheit. ▲ La côte de Block Island, Rhode Island, New York. Cette photo est extraite d'une série intitulée «American Moments», réalisée pour le compte de *Travel Holiday Magazine*. Bien que l'image ait été prise tard dans l'après-midi une journée de mai, l'atmosphère est hivernale et sombre, ce qui renforce l'impression de solitude et souligne la beauté de l'ensemble.

PAGE 165 Photographer: KENT BARKER Publisher/Client: *AMERICAN WAY MAGAZINE/AMERICAN AIRLINES* Camera: HASSELBLAD ELX Film: KODAK T-MAX 100 Art Director: KYLE DREIR Country: USA ■ The "Jantzen Swimmer" on the once popular Daytona Beach Boardwalk in Florida. This boardwalk and a few others are part of a rapidly vanishing landscape in the United States. In a photo essay for the in-flight magazine of American Airlines, the photographer captured the romance and nostalgia of these disappearing icons. ● «Jantzen-Schwimmerin» an der Promenade der einst sehr beliebten Daytona Beach in Florida. Hölzerne Uferpromenaden wie diese prägten früher die Strände der USA, heute sind sie selten geworden. In einem Photo-Essay für das Inflight-Magazin der American Airlines hielt der Photograph die Romantik und Nostalgie dieser rasch verschwindenden Ikonen fest. ▲ «La nageuse Jantzen» sur la célèbre Boardwalk de Daytona Beach en Floride. Jadis typiques des longues plages américaines, ces promenades formées de planches en bois sont aujourd'hui de plus en plus rares. Dans le cadre d'un reportage photo effectué pour un magazine d'American Airlines, le photographe fixa sur la pellicule le romantisme teinté de nostalgie de ces icônes appelées à disparaître.

PAGE 166 Photographer: STEVE RICHARDSON Representative: CHRISTINE RICHARDSON Client: NEENAH PAPER COMPANY Camera: MAMIYA 645 Film: ILFORD HP5 Exposure: F16/1/2 sec. Art Director: BOB KAY Agency: KAMSTRA COMMUNICATIONS Country: USA ■ Photo used in an ad for a paper manufacturer. In the middle of the Manistee National Forest on the shore of Lake Michigan, the photographer suddenly came across these rows of planted pine trees. The scene actually looked the way the black-and-white photograph shows. ● Diese Aufnahme wurde für die Anzeige eines Papierherstellers verwendet. Mitten in einem Waldstück am Michigansee stiess der Photograph ganz unerwartet auf Reihen neu angepflanzter Kiefern. Dieses Schwarzweissbild gibt die tatsächliche farbliche Stimmung der Szene exakt wieder. ▲ Cette photo fut utilisée pour la publicité d'un fabricant de papier. Au cœur d'une forêt qui borde le lac Michigan, le photographe découvrit par hasard de tout jeunes pins plantés en rangée. Ce cliché en noir et blanc reflète fidèlement l'atmosphère de la scène.

PAGE 167 Photographer: LES SZURKOWSKI Client: *STUDIO MAGAZINE* & KODAK CANADA Camera: NIKON F4s Film: EKTACHROME 100 Exposure: F22/1/8 sec. Country: CANADA ■ Image from a series entitled "Observations." The series explored the illusion of one's perception of two-dimensional photographic images. Typical, well-balanced images attract the viewer, but on closer analysis the viewer finds that the shots unveil an unusual element that does not belong. Here, the beach shot was taken in Puerto Angel, Mexico, while the set of bamboo sticks was shot at the beach in Puerto Escondido, 50 miles away. ● Das Bild gehört zu einer Reihe mit dem Titel «Beobachtungen». Thema war die Illusion der Wahrnehmung bei zweidimensionalen photographischen Bildern. Typische, in der Komposition ausgewogene Bilder ziehen den Betrachter an, der bei näherer Hinsicht aber ungewöhnliche Elemente entdeckt, die nicht ins Bild gehören. Bei diesem Bild wurden zwei Aufnahmen verwendet: Der Strand wurde in Puerto Angel, Mexiko, photographiert, die Bambusstämme am gleichen Tag 80km entfernt am Strand von Puerto Escondido. ▲ Image extraite d'une série intitulée «Observations» et consacré à l'illusion créée par le biais de photos bidimensionnelles. Typiques, ces images à la composition équilibrée, mais qui,

au second regard, laissent découvrir des éléments insolites. Deux prises de vue ont servi à la réalisation de ce montage: le cliché de la plage a été pris à Puerto Angel, au Mexique, tandis que les tiges de bambou ont été photographiées le même jour, 80km plus loin, sur la plage de Puerto Escondido.

PAGES 168, 169 Photographer: KLAUS D. FRANCKE Representative: BILDERBERG/ARCHIV DER FOTOGRAFEN Publisher: EDITION STEMMLE Designers: KLAUS D. FRANCKE, PETER WASSERMANN Country: GERMANY ■ Images from a book with aerial views of Iceland. Left: a small opening in the ice of the partly water-filled crater of the Grmsvötn volcano. Since the Middle Ages it has been Iceland's most active volcano. Right: hills in the Maelifell Sander with rivulets of melting water in the moss vegetation. ● Diese Aufnahmen stammen aus dem Buch *Island – Luftbilder*. Links ein kleiner See, der durch die Eis- und Schneeschmelze im Eis des teilweise wassergefüllten Kraters des Grmsvötn-Vulkans entstanden ist. Es ist der seit dem Mittelalter aktivste Vulkan Islands. Rechts: Hügel im Maelifell-Sander mit Schmelzwasserrinnsalen in der Moosvegetation. ▲ Ces photos sont extraites d'un livre de vues aériennes sur l'Islande. A gauche, un petit lac qui, lors de la fonte des neiges, s'est formé dans le cratère du volcan Grmsvötn, partiellement rempli d'eau. Ce volcan est, depuis le Moyen Age, le plus actif de l'île. A droite, collines du Maelifell-Sander, dont le tapis de mousse est sillonné de ruisselets à la fonte des neiges.

PAGES 170, 171 Photographer: KLAUS D. FRANCKE Representative: BILDERBERG/ARCHIV DER FOTOGRAFEN Publisher: EDITION STEMMLE Designers: KLAUS D. FRANCKE, PETER WASSERMANN Country: GERMANY ■ Further images from the photographer's book of aerial views of Iceland. At left: a small river in the Landeyjar Sander. Marram grass grows in the black sand of the spit. At right, top: a brooklet with high content of ferric oxide in a moor; bottom: a glacial streamlet in the Landeyjar Sander. ● Weitere Aufnahmen aus dem Buch *Island – Luftbilder*. Links ein kleiner Fluss im Landeyjar-Sander. Im schwarzen Sand der Nehrung wächst Strandhafer. Rechts oben: ein moorentwässernder Bach mit hohem Eisenoxydgehalt; unten ein Gletscherbach im Landeyjar-Sander. ▲ Autres images du livre de vues aériennes sur l'Islande. A gauche, petit cours d'eau du Landeyjar-Sander. De l'oyat pousse dans le sable noir du littoral. En haut à droite: un ruisseau à forte teneur en oxyde de fer dans un marais; en bas, torrent glaciaire dans le Landeyjar-Sander.

PAGE 172 Photographer: STEPHEN WILKES Representative: DOUG BROWN Designer: STEVE LISKA/LISKA & ASSOCIATES Camera: Nikon F4 Film: Fuji Velvia Country: USA ■ "Aerial Snorklers"—grab shot made over Maui, Hawaii. The couple's scale against the background caught the attention of the photographer, who used a long lens (300mm) to exaggerate the perspective. ● Diese Aufnahme entstand vor dem Maui Vulkan von Hawai. Der Photograph verwendete ein 300mm-Objektiv, um die Perspektive zu intensivieren. ▲ Prise de vue aérienne de deux plongeurs munis de leur tuba sur l'île Maui, Hawai. Le photographe a utilisé un objectif de 300mm afin d'obtenir cette perspective.

PAGE 173 Photographer: NADAV KANDER Representative: STOCKLAND MARTEL Client: GLENMORANGIE WHISKY Art Director: NIGEL ROSE Agency: TBWA HOLMES KNIGHT RITCHIE Country: GREAT BRITAIN ■ "A Drop of Tranquility." Images shot for a campaign on Glenmorangie Whisky. ● «Ein Tropfen Ruhe» – Bilder aus einer Kampagne für Glenmorangie Whisky. ▲ «Une goutte de volupté» – Images publiées dans le cadre d'une campagne publicitaire pour le whisky Glenmorangie.

PAGE 174 Photographer: ARMIN BUHL Camera: NIKON F3 Film: ILFORD FP4 Exposure: F16/60 Country: GERMANY ■ The Munich airport tower with ventilation pipes. The photographer chose a very low viewpoint, a wide-angle lens, and a red filter, and was helped out by a very low sun, to obtain this interpretation of proportions. ● Der Tower des Münchener Flughafens und Lüftungstürme. Der Photograph wählte einen sehr tiefen Standpunkt und benutzte ein Weitwinkelobjektiv und einen extremen Rotfilter, um die besondere Wirkung der Proportionen zu erreichen. Begünstigt wurde seine Absicht durch die tiefstehende Sonne. ▲ La tour de l'aéroport de Munich et des tours de ventilation. Pour obtenir cet effet de proportions spécial, le photographe a choisi de prendre son sujet en contre-plongée avec un grand-angle et un filtre rouge, le soleil se trouvant très bas à l'horizon.

PAGES 176, 177 Photographer: MICHAEL MELFORD Publisher/Client: *TRAVEL HOLIDAY MAGAZINE/READER'S DIGEST PUBLICATIONS* Camera: NIKON F4 Film: FUJI VELVIA Exposure: F11/1/2 sec., F8.5/1/4 sec. Director of Photography: BILL BLACK Art Director: LOU DILORENZO Photo Editor: STEPHANIE ANNE SYROP Photo Coordinator: SANDY PEREZ Country: USA ■ Images from a feature on Bermuda in *Travel Holiday Magazine*. The idea was to show the other side of Bermuda, not the usual touristic shots. At left: right after a thunderstorm, a special light colored the sky and the roof of the Reefs Hotel just long enough to take a few exposures. At right: the sun popped out just before setting, making the lighthouse appear in a spectacular light. ● Diese Aufnahmen stammen aus einem Beitrag über die Bermuda-Inseln in einer Reisezeitschrift. Die Idee war, nicht die üblichen Tourismusbilder zu zeigen. Links: Nach einem Gewitter erhellt ein spezielles Licht den Himmel und das Dach des Reefs Hotels. Rechts: Gerade vor Sonnenuntergang war die Sonne noch einmal durchgebrochen, und der Leuchtturm über den Dächern von Bermuda erschien in einem spektakulären Licht. ▲ Images des Bermudes extraites d'un magazine de voyages. A gauche: juste après un orage, une lumière extraordinaire baigne le ciel et le toit de l'hôtel Reefs. A droite: avant de s'éteindre sur l'horizon, le soleil refit une brève apparition pour irradier le phare de ses rayons.

PAGES 178, 179 Photographer: AERNOUT OVERBEEKE Representatives: CHRISTA KLUBERT, GERMANY; FREDDY BRAZIL, GREAT BRITAIN; HILARY BRADFORD, ITALY Camera: ROLLEIFLEX Film: KODAK TRI-X Art Director: AERNOUT OVERBEEKE Country: NETHERLANDS ■ At left: detail of a crane; at right: a sugar factory. In this series of personal work photographer Aernout Overbeeke turns away from his "large" landscapes to "small" still-life photos. (Also see following spread.) ● Links: Detail eines Krans; rechts: eine Zuckerfabrik. Mit dieser Reihe freier Arbeiten verlegt sich Aernout Overbeeke von den für ihn typischen «grossen» Landschaften auf «kleine» Stilleben. (Siehe auch die folgende Doppelseite.) ▲ A gauche: détail d'une grue; à droite: une fabrique de sucre. Avec cette série libre, le photographe Aernout Overbeeke a changé de registre, abandonnant ses «grands» paysages si typiques au profit de «petites» natures mortes. (Voir également la double page suivante.)

PAGES 180, 181 Photographer: AERNOUT OVERBEEKE Representatives: CHRISTA KLUBERT, GERMANY; FREDDY BRAZIL, GREAT BRITAIN; HILARY BRADFORD, ITALY Camera: ROLLEIFLEX Films: ILFORD XP2 (1), KODAK TRI-X (2) Country: NETHERLANDS ■ At left: part of an old industrial machine photographed in Belgium; at right: oil platform in Veslefrikk, Norway. ● Links: Detail einer alten Maschine (in Belgien aufgenommen); rechts: Ölbohrplattform in Veslefrikk, Norwegen. ▲ A gauche: détail d'une vieille machine industrielle (photographiée en Belgique); à droite: plate-forme pétrolière à Veslefrikk, Norvège.

PAGES 182, 183 Photographer: VIRGILE BERTRAND Camera: NIKON F3 Film: KODAK 100 PLUS Art Director: VIRGILE BERTRAND Country: FRANCE ■ Laundry shops, frequented mostly by singles and by families of low income or of no fixed abode, are places of waiting, of solitude, of passing by, in which everyone tries to protect his privacy from his neighbor. With strong visual elements like steam, the doors of the washers, and trolleys, the photographer captured the atmosphere with love and irony. He worked without montage or additional light, making use of the reflections lacquered areas, on the metal of the machines, or simply by working with this lens which was moistened partly to obtain the desired results. ● Waschsalons – sie werden vor allem von Singles, von Obdachlosen und von Familien mit sehr niedrigen Einkommen benutzt. Es sind Orte des Wartens, der Einsamkeit, des Durchgangs, wobei jeder seine Intimität (sprich Wäsche) vor dem Nachbarn zu schützen sucht. Mit stark konnotativen Elementen wie Dampf, Türen von Maschinen, Trommeln, Einkaufswagen fängt der Photograph die spezielle Atmosphäre auf liebevolle und ironische Art ein. Es sind Reportageaufnahmen, ohne Montage oder zusätzliches Licht. Der Photograph arbeitete nur mit den Lichtreflexionen auf Lackflächen, dem Metall der Maschinen oder er befeuchtete einfach das Objektiv stellenweise, um den gewünschten Effekt zu erzielen. ▲ Les laveries automatiques, destinées majoritairement à des célibataires, aux familles de revenus modestes, aux sans domicile fixe, sont dotées d'aménagements strictement fonctionnels, uniformisés. Il s'agit d'un lieu de solitude, de passage et d'attente, où chacun préserve son intimité (son linge) du voisinage immédiat. A travers ces images, le photographe s'est efforcé d'associer avec amour et ironie une multitude d'éléments immédiatement identifiables, aux fortes connotations: vapeur, portes de machine, tambours, chariots de supermarché... Aucune de ces photographies n'a été montée, toutes ont été prises en condition de reportage, sans aucun éclairage additionnel. Les imbrications et «effets» ont été obtenus en recherchant les moindres reflets sur les peintures laquées, l'inox des machines à laver ou, plus simplement, en embuant irrégulièrement l'objectif.

Pages 184, 185 Photographer: FRANCES MOCNIK Camera: MAMIYA 645 Film: ILFORD FP4 Exposure: F22/1/2 SEC. (184), F16/125 (185) Art Director: FRANCES MOCNIK Country:

AUSTRALIA ■ Mitchel Landscape I and II, Canberra, Australia. In the semi-urban, semi-industrial regions on the fringe of Canberra, the photographer discovered clear and distinct compositions of line, form, and shadow. Shooting during intense sunlight, he dealt with hard shadows and bright highlights that exceeded the scene luminance acceptance range of the film. As he wanted to retain both the shadow and highlight detail, he compressed the scene luminance range to that accepted by the film. Using Ilford FP4, he overexposed the film (in most cases by two stops) and underdeveloped the film (by two stops). The negatives were printed on grade 2 Ilford Multigrade Fibre Based Paper and toned with Selenium toner. ● Mitchel Landscape I und II, Canberra, Australien. Am Rande Canberras, in einem gemischten Wohn- und Industriequartier, entdeckte der Photograph aussergewöhnliche, klare Kompositionen von Linien, Formen und Schatten. Da er harte Schatten und Lichteffekte für seine Komposition brauchte, photographierte er bei starkem Sonnenlicht. Daraus resultierte ein zu starker Kontrastumfang für den Film. Um das Problem zu lösen, arbeitete er mit Überbelichtung des Ilford FP4-Films (meistens um zwei Blenden), den er danach um zwei Stufen reduziert entwickelte. Die Negative wurden auf Ilford Multigrade Fibre Based Paper abgezogen und mit Selenium getönt. ▲ Mitchel Landscape I et II, Canberra, Australie. Dans un quartier industriel et locatif de la banlieue de Canberra, les lignes, les formes et les ombres fondues dans des compositions pures et nettes ont arrêté l'œil du photographe. Comme il a réalisé sa prise de vue par un grand soleil, les contrastes entre les ombres, très dures, et les lumières, très vives, étaient trop forts pour la sensibilité de son film. Afin de garder des détails à la fois dans les noirs et dans les blancs, il a surexposé son film (Ilford FP-4) avant de le sous-exposer au développement. Les négatifs ont été tirés sur papier Ilford Multigrade Fibre Based et virés au sélénium.

PAGES 186, 187 Photographer: FRANÇOIS HALARD Representative: JEAN GABRIEL KAUSS Publisher/Client: *HARPER'S BAZAAR*/THE HEARST CORPORATION Camera: KONICA INSTANT PRESS Film: POLAROID Art Director: FABIEN BARON Country: USA ■ Images from an article that appeared in *Harper's Bazaar* on the restoration of a cottage in Maine. The owner, Judyth van Amringe, packed the cottage with furniture of her own design and objects collected from flea markets and auctions. ● Diese Bilder stammen aus einem Artikel in *Harper's Bazaar* über die Restaurierung eines kleinen Landhauses in Maine, USA. Die Eigentümerin, Judyth van Amringe, staffierte es mit selbst entworfenen Möbeln und Objekten von Flohmärkten und Auktionen aus. ▲ Ces images sont extraites d'un article publié dans *Harper's Bazaar*, consacré à la restauration d'une petite maison de campagne située dans le Maine, Etats-Unis. La propriétaire, Judyth van Amringe, l'a aménagé avec des meubles qu'elle a créés elle-même et des bibelots trouvés dans des brocantes ou des ventes aux enchères.

PAGE 188 Photographer: JOANNE DUGAN Client: NEW ALBION RECORDS Camera: NIKON F3 Film: KODAK INFRARED Exposure: F8/125 Art Director: TODD REAMON Country: USA ■ The portal of St. John the Divine in New York City, the world's largest Gothic cathedral. This image was part of an assignment for a CD cover for harmonic piano player Michael Harrison, whose playing technique is found in the music of ancient Greece, India, Persia, China, and Japan, yet sounds very modern. The image looks as if it could have been shot in any of those countries, either hundreds of years ago or just yesterday. Who would know that this was shot in one of the world's most urban areas? ● Das Portal der Kathedrale St. John The Divine in New York, der grössten gothischen Kathedrale der Welt. Das Bild gehört zu einem Auftrag für die Hülle einer CD des Pianisten Michael Harrison, dessen Technik auf der Musik des alten Griechenlands, Indiens, Persiens, Chinas und Japans beruht und trotzdem sehr modern klingt. Die Bilder sollten aussehen, als könnten sie in jedem dieser Länder vor hundert Jahren oder gerade gestern aufgenommen worden sein. Wer würde glauben, dass dieses Bild in einem so urbanen Umfeld entstand? ▲ Le portail de St. John The Divine à New York, la plus grande cathédrale gothique au monde. Cette image fait partie d'un projet pour la pochette CD du pianiste Michael Harrison, lequel s'inspire de la musique de la Grèce antique, de l'Inde, de la Perse, de la Chine et du Japon pour recréer un genre très moderne. Les clichés devaient donner l'impression d'avoir pu être pris dans n'importe lequel de ces pays, le jour même ou voici plusieurs siècles. Et qui penserait en effet qu'ils le furent dans l'un des environnements les plus urbains qui soient?

PAGE 189 Photographer: PETER ECKERT Camera: RAPID OMEGA Film: AGFAPAN 100 Exposure: 3 MIN. Country: USA ■ Union Station in Portland, a restored landmark. At night there is an eerie synergy of power. Idle and empty trains wait with generators running, lights on lonely platforms hum and flicker, and the station itself is lit up, although no one comes or goes. This image is part of a personal project of the photographer, exploring places that become visually unique at night. ● Der Bahnhof von Portland, ein restauriertes

Wahrzeichen der Stadt. Nachts entsteht ein eigenartiges Zusammenspiel von Elementen: abgestellte, leere Züge mit laufenden Generatoren, verlassene Bahnsteige mit summenden, flackernden Lichtern und der erleuchtete Bahnhof selbst, völlig menschenleer. Das Bild gehört zu einem persönlichen Projekt des Photographen und wurde nachts mit gewöhnlichem Schwarzweissfilm photographiert. ▲ La gare de Portland, emblème restauré de la ville. La nuit, les éléments exercent soudain un pouvoir surnaturel: comme désœuvrés, des trains vides attendent, générateurs en marche, tandis qu'une lumière vacillante éclaire les quais déserts et la gare, privée elle aussi de toute vie humaine. Cette photo est extraite d'un projet personnel du photographe qui explore les mystères de la nuit sur film noir et blanc.

PAGE 190 Photographer: MARTYN COLBECK Representative: OXFORD SCIENTIFIC FILMS LTD Camera: CANON EOS-1 Film: FUJICHROME VELVIA Country: GREAT BRITAIN ■ This photograph was taken in Amboseli National Park in Kenya. Martyn Colbeck, a freelance wildlife photographer and film-maker, has been documenting the lives of one particular family of elephants in Amboseli for two BBC documentary films, working closely with American scientist Cynthia Moss. He found this bull elephant dust bathing just after the sunrise, when the light from the low sun picked out every wrinkle of the elephant's skin in sharp detail. ● Diese Aufnahme entstand im Amboseli-Nationalpark von Kenya. Martyn Colbeck, freier Tierphotograph und Filmer, hat das Leben einer einzelnen Elefantenfamilie im Amboseli für zwei BBC-Filme dokumentiert. Dabei arbeitete er eng mit der amerikanischen Wissenschaftlerin Cynthia Moss zusammen. Er begegnete diesem Elefantenbullen beim morgentlichen Sandbad, kurz nach Sonnenaufgang, als das Licht der tiefen Sonne jede Kerbe der Elefantenhaut scharf nachzeichnete. ▲ Ces photos ont été prises au Kenya, dans le parc national Amboseli. Martyn Colbeck, photographe animalier indépendant et réalisateur de films, a suivi de près la vie d'une famille d'éléphants pour deux films documentaires de la BBC. Il collabora pour ce faire étroitement avec la scientifique américaine Cynthia Moss. Il rencontra cet éléphant mâle en train de prendre un bain de sable peu après le lever du jour, alors que la lumière du soleil éclairait nettement chaque pli et repli de la peau de l'animal.

PAGES 192, 193 Photographer: OLIVER MECKES Publisher/Client: STERN/GRUNER + JAHR Camera: R.E.M. JSJ 60 Film: AGFACHROME 100 RS Picture Editor: ELISABETH BIONDI Agency: KAGE INSTITUT FÜR WISSENSCHAFTLICHE FOTOGRAFIE Country: GERMANY ■ At left: the Ips typographus, the most common type of the notorious beetle; at right: the Melusina Ornata. With its pincers the beetle is able to break even hard wood fibers while the Melusina Ornata injects a substance with its bite that reduces bloodclotting, which can mean death to cattle. For the screen electrode micro shots, the insects had to be killed, fixed, dehydrated, and gilded. The photographs were shown in an article on the "Monsters of the Summer" in the magazine Stern. ● Der Buchdrucker, die häufigste Art des Borkenkäfers, und die Kriebelmücke. Der nur 4mm grosse Borkenkäfer knackt mit seinen Fresszangen auch harte Holzfasern; die Kriebelmücke, 3-4mm, injiziert beim Stechen einen Stoff, der die Blutgerinnung herabsetzt und für manche Rinder den Tod bedeutet. Für die Rasterelektronen-Mikroaufnahme mussten die Tiere getötet, fixiert, entwässert und vergoldet werden. Die Aufnahmen wurden in einem Beitrag mit dem Titel «Monster des Sommers» im Stern gezeigt. ▲ Le bostryche, une espèce de coléoptère très répandue, et la simulie. Long de 4 mm seulement, le bostryche s'attaque aux bois durs à l'aide de ses pinces, alors que la simulie – qui mesure 3 à 4 mm et s'avère particulièrement dangereuse pour le bétail – injecte en piquant une substance qui entrave la coagulation du sang, conséquence souvent mortelle pour l'animal. Pour cette photo effectuée avec un microscope électronique, les insectes ont préalablement été séchés, fixés et dorés. Ces photos illustraient un article publié dans le magazine Stern, intitulé «Les monstres de l'été».

PAGE 194 Photographer: BRUCE WEBER Representative: NAN BUSH Publisher: PEPE JEANS, LONDON Camera: PENTAX 6X7 Film: KODAK TRI-X Art Director/Designer: SAM SHAHID Agency: SHAHID AND CO. Country: GREAT BRITAIN ■ This lovely bull terrier was part of an ad for Pepe Jeans. ● Dieser wunderschöne Bullterrier gehört zu einer Anzeige für Pepe Jeans. ▲ Ce superbe bull-terrier fit partie d'une publicité pour les jeans Pepe.

PAGE 195 Photographer: JAMES SCHNEPF Representative: LINDA THOMSEN Client: SMITHFIELD FOODS Camera: HASSELBLAD Film: FUJICHROME 100 D Designer: JAMIE KOVAL Country: USA ■ Beauty portrait of a pig. This especially lean pig (the result of more than 20 years of ongoing genetic research and natural selection) was to be showcased for a food manufacturer. Compared to an average pig, it has a very calm disposition, but still the session was a test of patience. It was helped along by an experienced pig handler. ● Beauty-Aufnahme eines Schweines. Dieses ausgesprochen schlanke Schwein (das Ergebnis von 20 Jahren genetischer Forschung und natürlicher Zucht) sollte für einen Nahrungsmittelhersteller als Aufmacher seiner Information aufgenommen werden. Verglichen mit einem herkömmlichen Schwein hat es ein sehr ruhiges Temperament. Trotz dieser Tatsache und Beistand eines Experten im Umgang mit Schweinen, war die Aufnahme eine harte Geduldsprobe. ▲ Portrait d'un cochon. Particulièrement élancé, ce cochon provenant d'un élevage naturel est le résultat de 20 ans de recherches génétiques. Ce «portrait» était destiné à illustrer la campagne d'information d'un fabricant de produits alimentaires. Bien que réputé pour son tempérament plutôt conciliant, le sujet donna, malgré la présence d'un expert, bien du fil à retordre pendant la séance photo.

PAGE 196 Photographer: PHILIP DERENDORF Camera: NIKON FM2 Film: FUJI RVP Country: USA ■ "Cooling Rita"—the magic and beauty of symmetry caught with this shot of—part of—a dog cooling her stomach on a hot summer day. ● «Cooling Rita» – Zauber und Schönheit der Symmetrie, eingefangen mit dieser Aufnahme des Hinterteils einer Hündin, die an einem heissen Sommertag ihren Bauch kühlt. ▲ «Cooling Rita» – magie et beauté de la symétrie fixées sur cette image représentant l'arrière-train d'une chienne en train de se rafraîchir le ventre lors d'une chaude journée d'été.

PAGE 197 Photographer: DIRK FISCHER Camera: NIKON F4S Film: KODAK TRI-X PAN 800 Exposure: F5.6/1/8 SEC. Art Director/Designer: CHRISTIAN RIBBE Country: GERMANY ■ Location for this shot was the zoo of Hamburg, in the early evening. For his report on animals in the zoo, the photographer intended to make the elephant look like a stone sculpture and express the sadness of his unnatural condition. ● Aufnahmeort war der zoologische Garten in Hamburg in den frühen Abendstunden. Die Aufnahme entstand für eine Reportage über Zootiere. Um die Tristesse der unnatürlichen Lebensbedingungen des Elephanten auszudrücken, machte der Photograph ein steineres Symbol aus ihm. ▲ Prise en début de soirée dans le jardin zoologique de Hambourg, cette photo était destinée à illustrer un article sur les animaux en captivité. Changé en sculpture de pierre par le photographe, l'éléphant symbolise la tristesse et la cruauté d'un environnement en totale rupture avec les conditions de vie naturelles.

PAGE 198 Photographer: JOHNATHON ABRIELLE Publisher: BIG MAGAZINE Art Director: VINCE FROST Model: Oris Body Painting: EVELINN Country: SPAIN ■ Basketball player. ● Basketballspieler. ▲ Joueur de basket.

PAGE 200 Photographer: THE DOUGLAS BROTHERS Publisher: BIG MAGAZINE Camera: PENTAX 6X7 Film: TRI-X Designer: VINCE FROST Country: SPAIN ■ This image was shot in Mohammed Ali's old Gymnasium in Florida, which has since been demolished. ● Diese Aufnahme entstand in Muhammed Alis alter Boxhalle in Florida, die inzwischen abgerissen wurde. ▲ Photo prise en Floride, dans l'ancien gymnase de MohammedAli, démoli entre-temps.

PAGE 201 Photographer: JOHN HUET Representative: MARILYN CADENBACH ASSOCIATES Client: ADIDAS Camera: PENTAX 6X7 Film: KODAK TRI-X Art Director: STEVE DUNN Agency: LEAGAS DELANEY Country: USA ■ Image of a soccer player featured in Big Magazine. ● Porträt eines Fussballspielers für Big Magazine. ▲ Portrait d'un joueur de football pour Big Magazine.

PAGE 224 Photographer: NEAL BROWN Representative: SHARPE + ASSOCIATES Country: USA

CALL

FOR

ENTRIES

GRAPHIS **PHOTO** 97
ENTRY DEADLINE: AUGUST 31 1996

GRAPHIS **DESIGN** 97
ENTRY DEADLINE: NOVEMBER 30 1995

GRAPHIS **POSTER** 97
ENTRY DEADLINE: APRIL 30 1996

Graphis Photo 97 (Entry Deadline: August 31, 1996)

■ Ads, catalogs, invitations, announcements, record covers, and calendars on any subject. Photographs taken for consumer or trade magazines, newspapers, books and corporate publications. Personal studies on any subject. Experimental or student work on any subject. Eligibility: All work produced between September 1995 and August 1996. ● Anzeigen, Kataloge, Plattenhüllen, Kalender. Photos für Zeitschriften, Zeitungen, Bücher und Firmenpublikationen. Persönliche Studien. Experimentelle Aufnahmen oder Studentenarbeiten. In Frage kommen: Arbeiten, die zwischen September 1995 und August 1996 entstanden sind. ▲ Publicité, catalogues, invitations, annonces, pochettes de disques, calendriers. Reportages pour magazines et journaux, livres et publications d'entreprise. Études personnelles, créations expérimentales ou projets d'étudiants. Seront admis: tous les travaux réalisés entre septembre 1995 et août 1996.

Graphis Design 97 (Entry Deadline: November 30, 1995)

■ Ads; promotion brochures, catalogs, invitations, record covers, announcements, logos, corporate campaigns, calendars, books, book covers, packaging, company magazines; newspapers, consumer or trade magazines, annual reports; illustration. Eligibility: All work produced between December 1994 and November 1995. ● Werbung, Broschüren, Kataloge, Plattenhüllen, Logos, Firmenkampagnen, Kalender, Bücher, Buchumschläge, Packungen. Zeitschriften, Hauszeitschriften, Jahresberichte, Illustrationen. In Frage kommen: Arbeiten, die zwischen Dezember 1994 und November 1995 entstanden sind. ▲ Publicité; brochures, catalogues, invitations, pochettes de disques, annonces, logos, identité visuelle, calendriers, livres, packaging; journaux, revues, magazines de sociétés, rapports annuels; illustration. Seront admis: les travaux réalisés entre décembre 1994 et novembre 1995.

Graphis Poster 97 (Entry Deadline: April 30, 1996)

■ Advertising, cultural, and social posters. Eligibility: All work produced between May 1995 and April 1996. ● Plakate für Werbezwecke sowie kulturelle und soziale Plakate. In Frage kommen: Arbeiten, die zwischen Mai 1995 und April 1996 entstanden sind. ▲ Affiches publicitaires, culturelles et sociales. Seront admis: tous les travaux réalisés entre mai 1995 et avril 1996.

■ **What to send:** Reproduction-quality duplicate transparencies (4x5″ or 35mm). They are required for large, bulky or valuable pieces. ALL 35MM SLIDES MUST BE CARDBOARD-MOUNTED, NO GLASS SLIDE MOUNTS PLEASE! *Please mark the transparencies with your name.* If you do send printed pieces they should be unmounted. WE REGRET THAT ENTRIES CANNOT BE RETURNED. ● **Was einsenden:** Wenn immer möglich, schicken Sie uns bitte reproduktionsfähige Duplikatdias. *Bitte Dias mit Ihrem Namen versehen..* Bitte schicken Sie auf keinen Fall Originaldias. KLEINBILDDIAS BITTE IM KARTONRAHMEN, KEIN GLAS! Falls Sie uns das gedruckte Beispiel schicken, bitten wir Sie, dieses gut geschützt aber nicht aufgezogen zu senden. WIR BEDAUERN, DASS EINSENDUNGEN NICHT ZURÜCKGESCHICKT WERDEN KÖNNEN. ▲**Que nous envoyer:** Nous vous recommandons de nous faire parvenir de préférence des duplicata de diapositives (4x5″ ou 35mm. N'oubliez pas d'inscrire votre nom dessus). NE PAS ENVOYER DE DIAPOSITIVES SOUS VERRE! Si vous désirez envoyer des travaux imprimés, protégez-les, mais ne les montez pas sur carton. NOUS VOUS SIGNALONS QUE LES ENVOIS QUE VOUS NOUS AUREZ FAIT PARVENIR NE POURRONT VOUS ÊTRE RETOURNÉS.

■ **How to package your entry:** Please tape (do not glue) the completed entry form (or a copy) to the back of each piece. Please do not send anything by air freight. Write "No Commercial Value" on the package, and label it "Art for Contest." ● Wie und wohin senden: Bitte befestigen Sie das ausgefüllte Einsendeetikett (oder eine Kopie davon) mit Klebstreifen (nicht kleben) auf jeder Arbeit und legen Sie noch ein Doppel davon lose bei. Bitte auf keinen Fall Luft- oder Bahnfracht senden. Deklarieren Sie «Ohne jeden Handelswert» und «Arbeitsproben für Wettbewerb». ▲ Comment préparer votre envoi: Veuillez scotcher (ne pas coller) au dos de chaque spécimen les étiquettes dûment remplies. Nous vous prions également de faire un double de chaque étiquette, que vous joindrez à votre envoi, mais sans le coller ou le fixer. Ne nous expédiez rien en fret aérien. Indiquez «Sans aucune valeur commerciale» et «Echantillons pour concours».

■ **Entry fees:** Single entries: North America US$25; Germany DM 25,00; all other countries SFr 25.00. Three or more pieces entered in a single contest: North America US$65, Germany DM 65,00; all other countries SFr 65.00. **Students entry fees** (please send copy of student identification): US$15 for each single entry, US$35 for each campaign or series of three or more pieces entered in a single contest. ● **Einsendegebühren:** Für jede einzelne Arbeit: DM 25,00/SFr 25.00. Für jede Kampagne oder Serie von drei oder mehr Stück: DM 65,00/SFr 65.00. **Einsendegebühren für Studenten** (Ausweiskopie mitschicken): Für jede einzelne Arbeit: DM 15,00/SFr 15.00. Für jede Kampagne oder Serie von drei oder mehr Stück: DM 35,00/SFr 35.00. ▲**Droits d'admission:** Envoi d'un seul travail: US$ 25/SFr. 25.00. Campagne ou série de trois travaux ou plus pour un seul concours: US$ 65/SFr. 65.00. **Droits d'admission pour étudiants** (veuillez envoyer une photocopie de la carte d'étudiant): US$15/SFr. 15.00 pour un seul travail, $35/SFr. 35 pour chaque série de trois travaux ou plus.

■ **Where to send:** Entries from North America and Canada should be sent to the New York office and checks should be made payable to GRAPHIS US, INC, NEW YORK. Entries from all other countries should be sent to the Zurich office and checks should be made payable to GRAPHIS PRESS CORP., ZURICH. ● **Wohin senden:** Bitte senden Sie uns Ihre Arbeiten an Graphis Zürich zusammen mit einem Scheck, ausgestellt in SFr. (auf eine Schweizer Bank ziehen oder Eurocheck) oder überweisen Sie den Betrag auf PC Luzern 60-3520-6 oder PSchK Frankfurt 3000 57-602 (BLZ 50010060). ▲Où envoyer: Veuillez envoyer vos travaux à Graphis Zurich et joindre un chèque tiré sur une banque suisse ou un Eurochèque; ou verser le montant sur le compte chèque postal Lucerne 60–3520–6.

GRAPHIS PRESS, DUFOURSTRASSE 107, CH-8008 ZÜRICH, SWITZERLAND, TELEPHONE: 41-1-383 82 11, FAX: 41-1-383 16 43
GRAPHIS US, INC., 141 LEXINGTON AVENUE, NEW YORK, NY 10016, TELEPHONE: (212) 532 9387, FAX: (212) 213 3229

ENTRY FORMS

GRAPHIS **PHOTO** 97
ENTRY DEADLINE: AUGUST 31 1996

GRAPHIS **DESIGN** 97
ENTRY DEADLINE: NOVEMBER 30 1995

GRAPHIS **POSTER** 97
ENTRY DEADLINE: APRIL 30 1996

I WISH TO ENTER THE ATTACHED IN THE FOLLOWING GRAPHIS COMPETITION:

☐ **GRAPHIS POSTER** 97
(APRIL 30, 1996)

CATEGORY CODES

PO1 ADVERTISING
PO2 PROMOTIONAL
PO3 CULTURE
PO4 SOCIAL

☐ **GRAPHIS PHOTO** 97
(AUGUST 31, 1996)

CATEGORY CODES

PH1 FASHION
PH2 JOURNALISM
PH3 STILL LIFE
PH4 FOOD
PH5 PEOPLE
PH6 PRODUCTS
PH7 LANDSCAPES
PH8 ARCHITECTURE
PH9 WILD LIFE
PH10 SPORTS
PH11 FINE ART

☐ **GRAPHIS DESIGN** 97
(NOVEMBER 30, 1995)

CATEGORY CODES

DE1 BROCHURES
DE2 EDITORIAL
DE3 ILLUSTRATION
DE4 CORPORATE IDENTITY
DE5 PACKAGING
DE6 CALENDARS
DE7 CD/RECORD COVERS
DE8 BOOKS
DE9 MULTIMEDIA
DE10 MISCELLANEOUS

SENDER: CATEGORY CODE: _____

COMPANY _____

STREET _____

CITY/STATE _____   ZIP/COUNTRY _____

TELEPHONE _____   FAX _____

ART DIRECTOR: _____

COMPANY _____

STREET _____

CITY/STATE _____   ZIP/COUNTRY _____

TELEPHONE _____   FAX _____

DESIGNER: _____

COMPANY _____

STREET _____

CITY/STATE _____   ZIP/COUNTRY _____

TELEPHONE _____   FAX _____

PHOTOGRAPHER/ILLUSTRATOR: _____

STREET _____

CITY/STATE _____   ZIP/COUNTRY _____

TELEPHONE _____   FAX _____

DESIGN FIRM: _____

STREET _____

CITY/STATE _____   ZIP/COUNTRY _____

TELEPHONE _____   FAX _____

CLIENT: _____

STREET _____

CITY/STATE _____   ZIP/COUNTRY _____

TELEPHONE _____   FAX _____

I HEREBY GRANT PERMISSION FOR THE ATTACHED MATERIAL TO BE PUBLISHED FREE OF CHARGE IN ANY GRAPHIS BOOK, ARTICLE IN GRAPHIS MAGAZINE, OR ANY ADVERTISEMENT, BROCHURE OR OTHER MATERIAL PRODUCED FOR THE PURPOSE OF PROMOTING GRAPHIS PUBLICATIONS.

SIGNATURE _____   DATE _____

GRAPHIS PRESS, DUFOURSTRASSE 107, CH-8008 ZÜRICH, SWITZERLAND, TELEPHONE: 41-1-383 82 11, FAX: 41-1-383 16 43

GRAPHIS US, INC., 141 LEXINGTON AVENUE, NEW YORK, NY 10016, TELEPHONE: (212) 532 9387, FAX: (212) 213 3229

G R A P H I S   B O O K S

BOOK ORDER FORM: USA, CANADA, SOUTH AMERICA, ASIA, PACIFIC

BOOKS		ALL REGIONS
☐ GRAPHIS ADVERTISING 96	US$	69.95
☐ GRAPHIS ALTERNATIVE PHOTOGRAPHY 95	US$	69.95
☐ GRAPHIS ANNUAL REPORTS 4	US$	69.95
☐ GRAPHIS BOOK DESIGN	US$	75.95
☐ GRAPHIS CORPORATE IDENTITY 2	US$	75.95
☐ GRAPHIS DESIGN 96	US$	69.95
☐ GRAPHIS EPHEMERA	US$	75.95
☐ GRAPHIS FINE ART PHOTOGRAPHY	US$	85.00
☐ GRAPHIS INFORMATION ARCHITECTS	US$	69.95
☐ GRAPHIS MUSIC CDS	US$	75.95
☐ GRAPHIS NUDES	US$	89.95
☐ GRAPHIS PHOTO 95	US$	69.95
☐ GRAPHIS POSTER 95	US$	69.95
☐ GRAPHIS PRODUCTS BY DESIGN	US$	69.95
☐ GRAPHIS SHOPPING BAGS	US$	69.95
☐ GRAPHIS TYPOGRAPHY 1	US$	69.95
☐ GRAPHIS TYPE SPECIMENS	US$	49.95
☐ **GRAPHIS PAPER SPECIFIER SYSTEM (GPS)**	US$	395.00

** ADD $30 SHIPPING/HANDLING FOR GPS; AFTER DEC. 1, 1995, GPS IS $495.00

NOTE! NY RESIDENTS ADD 8.25% SALES TAX

☐ CHECK ENCLOSED (PAYABLE TO GRAPHIS)
(US$ ONLY, DRAWN ON A BANK IN THE USA)

USE CREDIT CARDS (DEBITED IN US DOLLARS)

☐ AMERICAN EXPRESS ☐ MASTERCARD ☐ VISA

CARD NO. _____ EXP. DATE _____

CARDHOLDER NAME _____

SIGNATURE _____

(PLEASE PRINT)

NAME _____

TITLE _____

COMPANY _____

ADDRESS _____

CITY _____

STATE/PROVINCE _____ ZIP CODE _____

COUNTRY _____

SEND ORDER FORM AND MAKE CHECK PAYABLE TO:
GRAPHIS US, INC.,
141 LEXINGTON AVENUE, NEW YORK, NY 10016-8193, USA

BOOK ORDER FORM: EUROPE, AFRICA, MIDDLE EAST

BOOKS	EUROPE/AFRICA MIDDLE EAST	GERMANY	U.K.
☐ GRAPHIS ADVERTISING 96	SFR. 123.–	DM 149,–	£ 52.00
☐ GRAPHIS ALTERNATIVE PHOTO 95	SFR. 123.–	DM 149,–	£ 52.00
☐ GRAPHIS ANNUAL REPORTS 4	SFR. 137.–	DM 162,–	£ 55.00
☐ GRAPHIS BOOK DESIGN	SFR. 137.–	DM 162,–	£ 55.00
☐ GRAPHIS CORPORATE IDENTITY 2	SFR. 137.–	DM 162,–	£ 55.00
☐ GRAPHIS DESIGN 96	SFR. 123.–	DM 149,–	£ 52.00
☐ GRAPHIS EPHEMERA	SFR. 137.–	DM 162,–	£ 55.00
☐ GRAPHIS FINE ART PHOTOGRAPHY	SFR. 128.–	DM 155,–	£ 69.00
☐ GRAPHIS INFORMATION ARCHITECTS	SFR. 123.–	DM 149,–	£ 52.00
☐ GRAPHIS MUSIC CDS	SFR. 137.–	DM 162,–	£ 55.00
☐ GRAPHIS NUDES	SFR. 168.–	DM 168,–	£ 62.00
☐ GRAPHIS PHOTO 95	SFR. 123.–	DM 149,–	£ 52.00
☐ GRAPHIS POSTER 95	SFR. 123.–	DM 149,–	£ 52.00
☐ GRAPHIS PRODUCTS BY DESIGN	SFR. 123.–	DM 149,–	£ 52.00
☐ GRAPHIS SHOPPING BAGS	SFR. 123.–	DM 149,–	£ 52.00
☐ GRAPHIS TYPOGRAPHY 1	SFR. 137.–	DM 162,–	£ 55.00
☐ GRAPHIS TYPE SPECIMENS	SFR. 75.–	DM 89,–	£ 37.00

(FOR ORDERS FROM EC COUNTRIES V.A.T. WILL BE CHARGED IN ADDITION TO ABOVE BOOK PRICES)

FOR CREDIT CARD PAYMENT (DEBITED IN SWISS FRANCS):
☐ AMERICAN EXPRESS   ☐ DINER'S CLUB
☐ VISA/BARCLAYCARD/CARTE BLEUE

CARD NO. _____ EXP. DATE _____

CARDHOLDER NAME _____

SIGNATURE _____

☐ PLEASE BILL ME (ADDITIONAL MAILING COSTS WILL BE CHARGED)

(PLEASE PRINT)

LAST NAME _____ FIRST NAME _____

TITLE _____

COMPANY _____

ADDRESS _____

CITY _____ POSTAL CODE _____

COUNTRY _____

PLEASE SEND ORDER FORM TO:
GRAPHIS PRESS CORP.
DUFOURSTRASSE 107, CH–8008 ZÜRICH, SWITZERLAND

GRAPHIS MAGAZINE